First published in Great Britain in 2005 by:
Triumph House
Remus House
Coltsfoot Drive
Peterborough
PE2 9JX
Telephone: 01733 898102
triumphhouse@forwardpress.co.uk
www.forwardpress.co.uk

HB ISBN 1-84431-084-1

Daily Reflections 2006

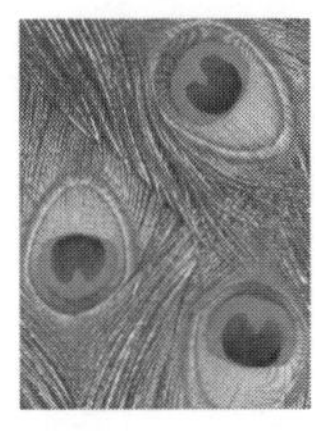

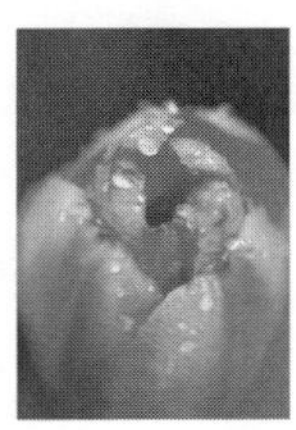

Triumph House
Daily Reflections

Daily Reflections
2006
Book Dedication

Foreword

This unique anthology offers an uplifting assortment of expressions in verse, musing on the physical, spiritual and emotional world we live in. Featuring works that can be enjoyed by all lovers of poetry to provide contemplation for every day of the year, each page holds an inspirational gem to brighten your mood.

The Triumph House editors have meticulously selected these poems from an abundance of entries to compile an anthology to cherish and enjoy for years to come. The talent of the authors to craft the language and express themselves, combined with their intuitive view of life, creates a series of enlightening compositions that have been a joy to work with.

Containing spiritually stimulating and thought-provoking words that will engage and charm, *Daily Reflections 2006* is a collection of enthralling literature to accompany you throughout the year ahead.

Heather Killingray
Editor

Contents

January

1st January 15
1st January 16
1st January 17
2nd January 18
2nd January 19
3rd January 20
4th January 21
5th January 22
6th January 23
6th January 24
7th January 25
7th January 26
8th January 27
9th January 28
9th January 29
10th January 30
11th January 31
12th January 32
12th January 33
13th January 34
13th January 35
14th January 36
15th January 37
16th January 38
17th January 39
18th January 40
19th January 41
20th January 42
21st January 43
22nd January 44
23rd January 45
24th January 46
24th January 47
25th January 48
25th January 49
26th January 50
26th January 51
27th January 52
27th January 53
28th January 54
28th January 55
29th January 56
30th January 57
31st January 58
31st January 59

February

1st February 60
2nd February 61
2nd February 62
3rd February 63
4th February 64
4th February 65
5th February 66
5th February 67
6th February 68
7th February 69
8th February 70
9th February 71
10th February 72
11th February 73
11th February 74
12th February 75
13th February 76
13th February 77
14th February 78
14th February 79
15th February 80
15th February 81
16th February 82
16th February 83
17th February 84
18th February 85
18th February 86
19th February 87
20th February 88
21st February 89
21st February 90
22nd February 91
23rd February 92
24th February 93
25th February 94
26th February 95
27th February 96
28th February 97

March

1st March 98
1st March 99
2nd March 100
2nd March 101
3rd March 102
4th March 103
4th March 104
5th March 105
6th March 106
6th March 107
7th March 108
8th March 109
8th March 110
9th March 111
9th March 112
10th March 113
11th March 114
11th March 115
12th March 116
13th March 117
14th March 118
15th March 119
16th March 120
17th March 121
18th March 122
19th March 123
20th March 124
21st March 125
22nd March 126
22nd March 127
23rd March 128
24th March 129
24th March 130
25th March 131
26th March 132
26th March 133
26th March 134
27th March 135
28th March 136
28th March 137
29th March 138
29th March 139
30st March 140
31st March 141
31st March 142

April

1st April 143
1st April 144
2nd April 145
3rd April 146
3rd April 147
4th April 148
4th April 149
5th April 150
6th April 151
7th April 152
8th April 153
8th April 154
9th April 155
10th April 156
11th April 157
11th April 158
12th April 159
12th April 160
12th April 161
13th April 162
13th April 163
14th April 164
14th April 165
15th April 166
15th April 167
16th April 168
16th April 169
16th April 170
17th April 171
18th April 172
19th April 173
19th April 174
20th April 175
21st April 176
21st April 177
22nd April 178
23rd April 179
23rd April 180
24th April 181
25th April 182
25th April 183
26th April 184
27th April 185
27th April 186
28th April 187
29th April 188
30th April 189

May

1st May 190
2nd May 191
3rd May 192
4th May 193
5th May 194
6th May 195
7th May 196
8th May 197
9th May 198
10th May 199
11th May 200
11th May 201
12th May 202
13th May 203
14th May 204
14th May 205
15th May 206
16th May 207
17th May 208
18th May 209
18th May 210
19th May 211
20th May 212
21st May 213
21st May 214
22nd May 215
23rd May 216
24th May 217
25th May 218
26th May 219
27th May 220
28th May 221
29th May 222
29th May 223
30th May 224
31st May 225

June

1st June 226
2nd June 227
3rd June 228
4th June 229
5th June 230
6th June 231
7th June 232
8th June 233
9th June 234
10th June 235
11th June 236
12th June 237
13th June 238
14th June 239
15th June 240
16th June 241
16th June 242
17th June 243
18th June 244
19th June 245
20th June 246
21st June 247
22nd June 248
23rd June 249
24th June 250
25th June 251
26th June 252
26th June 253
27th June 254
27th June 255
28th June 256
28th June 257
29th June 258
30th June 259
30th June 260

July

1st July	26
1st July	262
2nd July	263
2nd July	264
3rd July	265
3rd July	266
4th July	267
5th July	268
6th July	269
6th July	270
7th July	271
7th July	272
8th July	273
8th July	274
9th July	275
10th July	276
11th July	277
11th July	278
12th July	279
12th July	280
13th July	281
13th July	282
14th July	283
15th July	284
16th July	285
17th July	286
17th July	287
18th July	288
18th July	289
19th July	290
20th July	291
20th July	292
21st July	293
21st July	294
22nd July	295
23rd July	296
24th July	297
25th July	298
26th July	299
27th July	300
27th July	301
28th July	302
29th July	303
30th July	304
30th July	305
31st July	306
31st July	307

August

1st August	308
2nd August	309
2nd August	310
3rd August	311
4th August	312
5th August	313
5th August	314
6th August	315
7th August	316
8th August	317
9th August	318
10th August	319
11th August	320
12th August	321
12th August	322
13th August	323
13th August	324
14th August	325
15th August	326
16th August	327
17th August	328
17th August	329
18th August	330
18th August	331
19th August	332
20th August	333
20th August	334
20th August	335
21st August	336
22nd August	337
22nd August	338
23rd August	339
23rd August	340
24th August	341
25th August	342
25th August	343
26th August	344
26th August	345
27th August	346
28th August	347
29th August	348
30th August	349
31st August	350

September

1st September	351
2nd September	352
3rd September	353
4th September	354
5th September	355
5th September	356
6th September	357
7th September	358
8th September	359
9th September	360
10th September	361
11th September	362
11th September	363
12th September	364
12th September	365
13th September	366
13th September	367
14th September	368
15th September	369
15th September	370
16th September	371
17th September	372
17th September	373
18th September	374
18th September	375
19th September	376
19th September	377
20th September	378
21st September	379
22nd September	380
23rd September	381
24th September	382
24th September	383
25th September	384
25th September	385
26th September	386
27th September	387
27th September	388
28th September	389
29th September	390
30th September	391

October

1st October	392
2nd October	393
3rd October	394
4th October	395
4th October	396
5th October	397
5th October	398
6th October	399
6th October	400
7th October	401
7th October	402
8th October	403
8th October	404
9th October	405
10th October	406
10th October	407
11th October	408
11th October	409
12th October	410
12th October	411
13th October	412
14th October	413
14th October	414
15th October	415
16th October	416
17th October	417
17th October	418
18th October	419
19th October	420
19th October	421
20th October	422
20th October	423
21st October	424
21st October	425
22nd October	426
23rd October	427
24th October	428
24th October	429
25th October	430
26th October	431
26th October	432
27th October	433
27th October	434
28th October	435
29th October	436
30th October	437
31st October	438

November

1st November	439
2nd November	440
3rd November	441
4th November	442
5th November	443
5th November	444
6th November	445
7th November	446
8th November	447
8th November	448
9th November	449
9th November	450
10th November	451
11th November	452
11th November	453
12th November	454
12th November	455
13th November	456
14th November	457
14th November	458
15th November	459
16th November	460
17th November	461
18th November	462
19th November	463
19th November	464
20th November	465
21st November	466
22nd November	467
23rd November	468
24th November	469
25th November	470
26th November	471
27th November	472
27th November	473
28th November	474
29th November	475
30th November	476

December

1st December	477
2nd December	478
3rd December	479
4th December	480
5th December	481
6th December	482
7th December	483
8th December	484
9th December	485
10th December	486
11th December	487
12th December	488
12th December	489
13th December	490
14th December	491
15th December	492
16th December	493
17th December	494
18th December	495
19th December	496
20th December	497
20th December	498
21st December	499
21st December	500
21st December	501
22nd December	502
22nd December	503
23rd December	504
23rd December	505
24th December	506
24th December	507
25th December	508
25th December	509
25th December	510
26th December	511
26th December	512
27th December	513
28th December	514
29th December	515
29th December	516
30th December	517
31st December	518
31st December	519
31st December	520

Other

A to Z of Authors	525
Information	530

Daily Reflections 2006

Poems, Thoughts & Reflections

Triumph House
Daily Reflections

1st January

New Year's Prayer

Sitting on her grandfather's chair
A little girl said a prayer
For those who do not have enough to eat,
Bring them a New Year filled with meat,
For those who do not have a home,
Give them solace from the storm,
For those who are wet and cold,
Give them a warm hand that they can hold,
For those in slavery
For their bravery,
May they be set free,
For it matters much to me.
With this, the child cast a tear,
For a world filled with fear,
She laid down her sleepy head,
Please keep the children safe and fed.
With these words she went to bed,
Do you think we've learnt instead?

Alan Pow

Moving On

Time to close this chapter
Time to move along
Time to make a fresh start
Time to prove them wrong

Start your life again now
Start it with some aim
Start to make a difference
Start to win the game

Believe in those around you
Believe in those who care
Believe you have a purpose
Believe that life is fair

Never see the same faults
Never live the past
Never take the easy way
Never walk too fast

Always share your troubles
Always lend your ears
Always listen good and well
Always show the tears

Believe you are a good friend
Believe you know the way
Believe in love and life itself
Believe and be okay

Sam Kelly

Internal Insight

(James 4:8, John 14:27, Rev 1:18)

Dawn has begun another day,
'I'm sad and lonely', what more can I say?
Weather is dreary, outdoors is windblown,
Cheery neighbours are jovial, and I want to moan.

It crossed my mind, something I'd read
In 'Daily Reflections' which had stuck in my head.
'Draw near to God and He'll draw near to you'.
I'd forgotten to trust Him. Rebuked - commitment was crucially renewed.

Renewing of personal faith, confessing faults,
Drawing near to The One who promised to blot
All fears and loneliness out of my life,
Brightening the gloom which threatened to blight.

Jesus was brave when facing His foes,
His strength was obtained from the Father who knows
Every situation, and circumstance we face.
He's able to deliver with abundant grace.

If nobody realises our personal state
Jesus is alive, and we know it. There's no debate.
Living each day under His control,
Bright spots and dull areas become mingled and His presence is continually bestowed.

Thanks to The One who understands our lot
Omnipresent, omnipotent, Omniscient is He, a mind-boggling thought.
A sense of humour is evident, no doubt about that
Just imagine our houseboat berthing at the quayside on Mount Ararat.

Annie R Harcus

Happy New Year

Every time a new year starts
Our minds go back to the year just past,
Some things were good and some were bad,
So will this one be the best we've had?

At midnight when the clock strikes out,
And we all sing Auld Lang Syne,
We make a wish and usually
Give a kiss to those we love
And raise our glasses high above.

We promise things we know full well
That we will never do,
But emotions are high,
And we truly believe
We can reach for the sky.

The next day dawns,
And we crawl out of bed,
Our feet touch the ground
But our head feels like lead.

What were those things
We said we would do?
Thank goodness we
Haven't got a clue.

Joan Brooks

2nd January

The Morning

The reddened sun and sky kissed
In the dawn's early rising mist
Lulled fields of early morn
Another day is being born
Silence dulled, across acres
To wake the early morning walkers
The glorious dawn calls
As dusk vanishes and falls
Comes the dawn chorus of the singing birds
In the field of gathering herds
Cows walk in rows, to milking time
The farmer breathes the fresh air and feels fine
Bleating sheep echo in the dullness
As the sun rises to its fullness
The cockerel crows, as if to wake
To announce daybreak
And the world stretches its arms
To the ringing of clocks' alarms
Once again the morning sleep does spoil
Starting the task of daily toil
Then comes the groaning traffic, set in lines
Beating to the railway times
Hustle and bustle of a working day begins
As workers earn their wages for their sins
The city wakes, and drones
Traffic honks, and moans
Crowds rush around amok
The day started in a shock
Comes that busy day
Work, earn, eat and pay.

Terry J Powell

3rd January

New Year Thoughts

A brand new year, a brand new day, what will the future bring?
Joy, hope, some trepidation, hands crossed as 'Auld Lang Syne' we sing.
Our thoughts wing back and memories jostle quickly through our minds
Eyes glisten unshed tears as the old year slips behind.
We stand upon the threshold as the new year lies ahead,
A prayer, our faith, the hand of God, as along life's path we're led.
We kiss, we hug, wish happiness and health the coming whole year through,
Trusting life will be benevolent as our resolutions we make anew.
We yearn for peace throughout the world, enough food for all to share,
For leaders to talk for some reprieve, and to display some care,
To do some good, help someone along and when each day is done,
Our prayers, our beliefs, God's encircling love is for each and every one.

Marjorie Leyshon

New Year's Day

Standing stock still
Like polished granite
Another monument to death,
Among the many
On a frosty New Year's day.

No greeting invited or given
Alone with his thoughts
As though communing with the dead.
On a frosty New Year's day.

Trees in sympathetic black
Against a leaden sky.
Adding weight to the burden of grief.
Hopelessness etched large
On a frosty New Year's day.

But with the trumpet's sound
And the archangel's shout
The dead will rise first!
In Christ, hope for the hopeless
On a frosty New Year's day.

Gordon Harper

Reunion

Tenderly, he picks his way gently through the forest of my mind. Slowly, he produces thoughts and feelings I thought were gone forever. Traumatised and reeling from shock he shifts into gear, positive and will be alerted to go into motivation.

Everything is made splendid, uncovering the dross of years and years. It is a tease in as much as the blind has not quite been lifted. But the promise it purveys should keep me in motivation until it all dissolves into history.

Barbara Rumsey

6th January

Daffodil

Daffodil lifts up her head,
Rises from her winter bed,
Dons a gown of gold and green,
Steps out gaily to be seen.
In field, hedgerow and garden,
At the roadside too,
Her brightly shining beauty
Displays for all to view.
With her siblings, crowds together,
Surviving vagaries of weather,
As her radiant beauty fades,
Leaves the centre of the stage,
To rest, restore and re-coup,
Next year the limelight
She'll once more scoop.

Sue Cann

6th January

Untitled

The wise men from the East followed a heavenly light, seeking a baby or toddler, vulnerable, dependent, innocent. It involved a long, hard and dangerous journey.

Eventually, probably after many months, the light was there blazing away over a humble, crowded and noisy place. This light also flooded their lives with joy and they went home changed forever.

'In Thy light we are bathed in light' (Ps36)

Caroline Pybus

7th January

Sweetness

When flowers grow at the end of winter
There is a sweetness to be found
From beneath a snowy velvet
They grow without a sound.
Crocus, snowdrops, purple pansies
Beauty formed in colourful array
Cherish the moment for you are seeing
Miracles of God in proud display
God is Spirit; He is love
God grows His seeds every day
The world's a garden you can be sure of
Calm, serenity, challenge violence and disarray
Bless you, bless you, bless each moment
May the world be bright each day
With the help of tiny flowers
Reflect my thoughts and my love's conveyed.

Christine Renee Parker

7th January

Breakfast With Frost

Sunday, late arising
Sitting, awaiting for Frost,
Eating and earnestly inhibiting
Mentally digesting, nothing lost.

Kitchen table, through television,
Frost, our earnest guide
Iraq, this Sunday, voting by the millions
Sad dam; democracy in stride?

Telegraph, six flaps through the letter slot
On vision, national newspaper analysis, Frost led,
Home and worldwide developments, such a knot
Individual specialists wide world tread.

I'd really feel helped if my Sunday Telegraph
(Laid aside on the breakfast table)
Could assist with my paragraph
A small area of blankness - if capable.

James R Lucas

8th January

A Helping Hand

On days when you feel down;
When no one else around,
Can comfort you or cheer you up,
Or wipe away your frown.

When things you'd like don't happen,
The way you'd want them to;
The skies are grey, day after day
And there seems no hope in view.

When troubles weigh so heavily,
You cannot sort them out,
Without some help, someone to share
These burdens of self-doubt.

Humble yourself before the Lord,
For He is always there,
In times like these, His love exceeds
As He listens to your prayer.

Pure white love He'll send you,
To lift your weary heart,
So trust in Him, you will begin
To make a fresh new start.

Tracey Lynn Birchall

9th January

The Little Snowdrop

Hello! It's me, I think I'm the first
For out of my bud I've only just burst.
It's a little cold, but the sun's on my face
I'm delicately nodding, I'm so full of grace.

Sometimes I'm up to my neck in the snow,
Sometimes on my face, the north wind will blow,
But when the sun shines and I look up to the sky,
I know my true meaning, yes, I know why.

Everybody loves me on a gloomy winter's day,
When my friends and I come out to play.
With my pretty white hat and my dress, oh so green,
I'm the first in the garden, the one to be seen.

I survived the winter, the cold, dismal days,
Now I come to life with the sun's rays.
I struggled thro' the earth, so frosty and cold,
Bringing light and bringing hope as I stand here so bold.

So remember me when life is unkind,
When your mind shuts down and your eyes are blind.
You'll struggle thro' and one day you will find
Your heart will open and so will your mind.

Glenys Harris

9th January

Actions Or Words?

In Your house, dear Lord,
Amongst my friends
I can happily state with conviction
All that You mean to me.
But out there in the wider world
Where scornfully labelled 'God Botherer'
I find it so difficult to proclaim my faith.
Then I think of Your words
To encourage Your disciples -
That it is through actions as well as words
People will see I follow You,
So whatever I can do for others
I can do it as for You;
Give me the necessary ability
And opportunity, I pray.

Di Bagshawe

Never Went Away

Come to me, be mine,
For I have waited a long time.
I cannot get you out of my mind.
You're there all night and day,
Love will not fade away.
In my heart you will stay.
Your love is mine.
In this big world I can see,
You have waited just for me.
I must be getting old, silly me.

Beryl Elizabeth Moore

11th January

Windowpane Thoughts

View winter with summer spirits,
Window gaze the weather,
See the falling snowflakes,
Similar to little ice pattern feathers.
Gosh the winter comes late,
Turn up the central heating,
Focus one's gaze on the crocuses,
The crocuses closed their heads; gone to sleep.
View then with summer spirit,
Thoughts of summer hours,
God's wonderful sunshine flowers,
Thoughts through a windowpane,
View winter with the summer spirits.

B G Clarke

Winter White

Pure winter white, winter light blue and bright
Fingered through blackened night
Chiselled features of your icy grasp, king of spades, queen of hearts
Bound into a glassy glaze, rounded by a frosty knave
That likens to the buds of May, makes them droop and
Makes them stare into a bleak future, an empty fare

Sheepish grins of little lambs, jigging, stamping,
Sprightly through an armoured land
And through the cold midnight hour,
Jack Frost will plan and edge his power
And govern every brassy pride that dreams of sunny summertime

Tracing beauty into sticky spring to harbour every living thing
While Einstein slumbers in his plot and tortoise doesn't give a jot
Concepts hibernate enjoined to last to every creature's living past

Naughty knave naive and hooked to all the frozen banks and brooks
Rendered power to churlish master
Girlish pride and children's laughter

Forgive my frozen empty soul
Brazen, unforgiving, thoughtless trodden
Clogging thought soured and rotten
Pristine likeness make no sound
Image bright to you I'm bound.

Ruth Toy

12th January

Today

What may today bring forth, I ask
What does this day hold new for me?
As I move from task to task
My inward eye has more to see
Than dirty dishes and pots and pans
And clothes that need a wash and spin
The untidy rooms - left all in a rush
By youthful, lively kith and kin.

All is peaceful - all is quiet
This is my time to think as I like
I do not need to travel far
For as I clean and tidy rooms
My mind and heart can fly for miles
And visit friends in distant lands
I hear their voices - see their smiles
While the duster's in my hands.

All I need is here within
Family portraits line the shelves
Memories dear lie in my heart
Who needs abundant jewels or wealth?
Much more precious to have good health
Someone to love and one to care
These are all beyond compare.

Joyce Beard

13th January

Pending

Such a variety of people we meet, while living on this Earth
And some influence us greatly, for better or for worse
We can all use our discretion and choose what's right or wrong
And if we've made some errors, put the blame where it belongs.
Our thoughts make constant changes, in our daily points of view
Sometimes the fronts of newspapers display some evil news.
Thank God for all the good things for they outweigh the bad
They fill our lives with happiness and banish what is sad.
We are not a lot of robots, made by some master up above,
Free will is what we're given, so let's fill the world with love.
We all have different troubles while we're living on this Earth,
So give out the hand of friendship, there's always someone worse.
A smile is like a tonic when you meet someone that's down,
Listen to their troubles and help remove their frown.
To really care for someone makes your troubles seem far less
And when this life is over, you'll know that you've been blessed.

Joan Prentice

Fear

You know me well, I've walked with you through all your lonely years
And yet, although you know me well, I still live off your fears
You push away the thoughts I give; the feelings I portray
Yet through your protests over time I manage to remain

But there are times when you escape and live your life carefree
But in the corners I still lurk. You're never free of me
Out of the darkness I can spring when you are feeling well
And I can drag you into depths of your own personal Hell

I live with you, I'm part of you. I never fully leave
Although at times I'd laid to rest, my spiderweb I weave
You cannot rub me from your life. I live inside your mind
You try to cut the bonds once more but once again I bind

Not just at night when all alone, when you have time to sleep
I'm with you when the day is light, your company I keep
I've played with you. You've been my friend. You give me so much joy
I twist the knife, the cuts are deep. You are my only toy

Just as love is part of you, as joy and hate and grief
Embrace me as an evil friend. From me there's no relief
As you grow old and weak of limb and on to death you wend
Look at me with kindly eyes, I'm with you to the end

Jennifer Davey

The Womb Of Youth

(Time will say nothing but I told you so,
Time only knows the price we have to pay;
If I could tell you I would let you know' - W H Auden (1940) 'But I Can't)

Jostled from the cool red
frothing placenta of youth,
she woke in the night's apocalypse
dancing to its rhythm 'n' blues.

The slender lithe torso whipped
her toes across the stars
as I sat to watch, with butterflies
caged inside my heart.

Now we are aged and lingering,
ruffled by nature's fingertips,
our pallor, as white as edelweiss
with the taste of Heaven on our lips.

Where we once danced the habanera
and our flesh blazed a sun-kissed hue,
we now bid adieus to the raging
waters of childhood's womb.

James McConalogue

15th January

I'm Your Friend

No matter how you feel,
You aren't alone.
As scared as you are,
I'll always be here to support you.
Never feel like there's no one you can turn to,
Because there is.
I'm your friend,
And I'll help you in any way you need.
Whether it's a hug and a shoulder to cry on,
Or a bottle of vodka and a litre of ice cream.
I care and I worry
And I'll never leave.

Colette Horsburgh

Hope

There's always light,
There's always light,
At the end
At the end of a dark tunnel.

The darkest night
Is always relieved,
By the spark
By the spark of the tiniest star.

In the blackest hole,
Deep underground,
Where day
Where day never meets night,

The full flower
From a candle flame,
Gives warmth
Gives warmth and comforts the soul.

In a lonely cupboard,
Under a sloping stair,
A sliver of silver
A sliver of silver lances the Stygian air.

To the dawn of a new day,
To the spring of a new year,
Hope rings out
Hope rings out
Dispelling heartache and fear.

L E Growney

17th January

Words

Words can be a weapon
Mightier than the sword
We cause fear and heartache
With just one angry word
Life - sometimes a burden
We live from day to day
Kind words help to make it easy
As we travel on our way
Words can give such power to hurt
To make us strong or weak
Remember words can't be revoked
Think well before you speak
Words can bring us happiness
To last throughout the years
Laughter, joy and sadness
Or banish all our fears
When you provoke someone to anger
If you make somebody cry
Too late to say you're sorry
When their last word is goodbye.

Lydia Barnett

18th January

The Power Of Laughter

Laughter is a sign of health
a sign of inner balance, inner peace
an ability to live in harmony with everything else

You cannot but only smile
when looking at the Creator's work - the beauty
of the Universe, including our Earth

You cannot but only laugh
when enjoying His work starting with your own
beauty

Laughing prolongs the life
why not to prolong your own life by admiring
your own beauty?

Discover yourself - the one and only masterpiece - unique in its kind!
and
you will live a long life full of laughter and smiles!

Vineta Svelch

19th January

Variation On A Theme

Like fluttering fingers brushing Braille,
My thoughts touch lightly, Lord my God,
The Heaven Your hands have made, have done.
As You emerge, no longer shades of shadows,
Wonder fills and brightens all my soul.

With all my words I cannot speak it
Half so clearly as the planets and the stars
Which, like a potter's wheel
(Proclaiming glory! with no words at all)
Spin round the Earth, that unrepentantly receives
Your sacrifice and love.

Tight across the earth, the sky
Like tautened canvas arches, dewed with stars.
A shining garden, frosted unripe silver by the moon
With lended light, until the sun, obedient to Your word,
Touches Earth's ripening rim, and rises.

Moonlight is so cold, my Lord.
The garden grows no balm, no healing herbs.
And is it empty of Your love for all eternity?
I am at Your gate, my Lord -
An anxious child, uncertain and unsure,
Unsure and faltering.

Richard Hain

The Inner Light

Still, quiet
unfathomable
darkness
rhythmic breathing
steady heartbeat
the kingdom of Heaven
lies truly within

Childlike, trusting
unseen union
valued solitude
watching, waiting.
Light in darkness
lifts the veil
an inner light.

Greta Robinson

21st January

Talking of you again
made the clouds of dreams fall apart ...
- years of laughter modify the soul (repeat ...)
who said that
steel is made of knowledge ... was it me?
Guess I was wrong in reading the books,
listening the language of the rain ...

A single kiss could never wake up
the sleepy ones
- years of pain modify the soul (repeat ...)

Opening the darkness
by silken fingers only ... the trace of
something sweet on the pillow,
your shoulder touching the skin ...
placing the cheeks in the power of your silence.
Who said
that love is the privilege of the wise? Was it you ...
guess you were right
- years of ... years ... modify ... everything ...

the repetition remains.

Jasmina Trifunovic

22nd January

Winged Spirit

Inspired thoughts are born on the
wings of the spirits of knowledge and imagination

Thought-provoking from many moons past
an idea cast by the wayside - forgotten
a tiny nucleus starts to formulate
motivation begins to awaken

Inspiration comes from imagination
imagination is fed by knowledge
knowledge is gained by learning
learning is brought about by experience
experience can be called upon for inspiration

So let your spirit free - live only your
own dreams - no one else's
follow your heart with courage
reap what you have sown and flourished
be inspired - be uplifted - it's yours

David Charles

23rd January

For All The Lonely

Do not despair that love will come
For often it lurks in funny places.
Smile and think how lucky you are
Able to work, walk, and talk to strange faces.
So get out and about, talk to all you meet.
Soon you will find friends that are keen,
To make your life happy again, as you smile,
Then life will seem brighter than it's ever been.

Marjorie Busby

24th January

Is There Life Beyond?

When you lose one parent you still have hope,
When you lose the second you think, *how will I cope?*
Suddenly you realise that those you love will leave
And you will be left, lost and lonely, to grieve,
For no one can truly share another's sorrow
Though kind friends will say, 'There's always tomorrow.'
For you finally comprehend what the end will be,
Goodbye to all you have known and seen
And what will there be to take its place,
Will you continue to exist in an altered state?
The greatest of the mysteries of human life -
At the moment of death will we see a white light,
Will we pass through a tunnel to another plane,
Will we dwell with former loved ones again
Or will we remain invisible to all
And act as guardians to those who call
Or will our spirits simply be reborn
In another body, another life form?

Christine Naylor

24th January

There Is Hope

All around us in this world, there are problems,
We see wars and changing times
Many question why bad things happen to good people,
Some have no joy, or real peace of mind.

When we have the Lord in our life,
We don't have to worry or be dismayed,
We have His promise of peace,
And of eternal rest and joy one day.

What a great hope it is to know,
'Jesus will always be there'
There is no problem you may have,
Which with Him, you cannot share.

Nothing is too difficult,
For our Loving God to do,
What He has done for others,
I know He will do for you.

There is peace in the midst of the storm,
For all who trust and walk by faith,
In the trials of this life, we thank God for Jesus;
He is the only true and lasting way.

There will be peace in the valley,
We shall dwell eternally with our Lord.
Child of God, 'Hold on by faith,
You are one day closer to your final reward.'

JoAnn P Kelly

25th January

Positive, Profound Statements

Time is one factor that creates a true friend,
Love and purity are to wrap this special gift,
Communication, trust, honesty and faith tie the wrapping,
Concrete this unique being.

With the soul comes the body (the spirit's temple),
And with the mind come thoughts unique!
(A true gift to share.)

Life should be concentrated on the positives,
And not be diluted by the negatives!
Or one could find one's self,
Missing out on how great life can be.

To gain one's self high in life,
Beat your own potential!
How does one do this?
Take hold and strive for what you have never known.

Judge not at what you see,
But ask why ... ?

Time will unfold what is to be,
And a choice of your own,
On how you will conduct your future's path.

A hum of your essence,
So unique as its form,
A joy to hear ...

To find clarity within,
Life's hurdles become simplistic,
To what has been clouded of the past ...

Don't change for another's vision,
Of what you might think should be ...

Lee Mak

25th January

Reflections

When you look into the mirror
And you look upon your face,
Do you see a true reflection of yourself?
Can you see the love of Jesus?
Does it radiate His love?
Or is there something else there in its place?

Is it full of love or hatred?
Does it show no signs of peace?
Can you see a little envy hiding there?
Is there bitterness just lurking
In some place you cannot see?
Are you really, really looking at your face?

Is it real, and is it true?
Does it show just who you are?
Or is it just another mask to hide behind?
When you look into that mirror
And gaze upon that face
Do you see a true reflection of yourself?

If you don't see love, but hatred,
If you don't see signs of peace
And the look of envy's hiding somewhere there
Look again, but much more closely
That is all that God will ask,
Just put the love of Jesus in its place.

George Terry

My Yesterday

My yesterday was so miserable
With gloomy memories, and places,
Like a sad story with a sad title,
Like a ewer broken into pieces.

My yesterday tries to put me to the test -
A letter in the drawer, a book on the desk -
They're still like a bullet piercing my breast ...
Yet, today my yesterday seems grotesque.

Yesterday I touched the bottom of despair -
Mad and dark - I'll let it repeat never!
My yesterday disappeared somewhere ...
Today's morning was truer and wiser.

Now I'm strong - it's unbelievable!
I feel regular beating of my heart.
It's summer! No tear and no trouble!
Goodbye yesterday! The sun is so bright ...

Jolanta Gradowicz

26th January

The Servant

(Dedicated to Vocations Sunday)

The servant, waited upon the Master,
The Master and His Mother,
Accepted the servant's service,
And rewarded, all servants with -
Eternal life.
The servant, lived a life,
Of service,
For the Master and His Mother,
Jesus and Mary.
The servant, had many roles,
Because the servant,
Became not one, but many.
These many, became,
Priests, Nuns, Sisters, Brothers
And Lay-workers.
All served God - with love.
Will you be a servant,
And serve God and Mary,
With love?

E B Wreede

Dreams

Sharp dreams about hunting the bear
The bear hiding in the tall bushes
A bad dream to dream about the bear
About the bear of the night
About a magical bear I cannot see
In the tall bushes of the night
A dream about hunting the bear
A dream about dreaming of the fox
A dream about a screaming fox
Bearer of bad omen
A dream about the woodpecker
A woodpecker pounding the home
A warning dream of death.

Mariana Zavati Gardner

27th January

The Power Of Meditation

Gently carried in the breeze of timeless meditations,
hungering, thirsting for my own release,
it lies just beyond the fallen shadows of my inner reflections.
Oh yes, my flames are ignited within,
stirring up its fire, time and time again.

I close my eyes, with my mind's power, I do clearly see -
my beating heart is constantly, continually inspired.
New beginnings, other worlds, and alternate dimensions,
spilling the power of my imaginations,
creating my heart's own ascension.

There, the birth of simplicity comes by merely believing,
even in agony's own silence, my heart is receiving.
Oh yes, all within that one gentle breeze
that carries my timeless reflections,
yes, there in the presence of my solitude and meditations.

Cathy L Kaiser

The Lord's Day

The day of the Lord is upon us
the light of His love warms my heart
for the joy of His word
wherever it's heard
has strengthened my soul from the start.

The peace of the Lord is upon us
His grace heals the scars on my heart
for the calm of His love
that flows from above
has nourished my soul from the start.

The joy of the Lord is upon us
His wonder alights in my heart
for His wonderful peace
that never will cease
has cherished my soul from the start.

The hope of the Lord is within me
His mercy has washed clean my heart
so the burden of sin
has been cleansed from within
and readied me for a new start.

Now the love of the Lord has enfolded me
and set a new beat to my heart
as I know through His love
He'll take me home above
for in His kingdom we never will part.

Daphne Cornell

28th January

The Antidote

(Most people lead lives of quiet desperation. Emerson)

Yes, this is so, though seldom they admit it,
Despair assails and seldom they outwit it,
Of mental states depression is the common cold,
Afflicting like some squalid, greasy mould.

For sure, it is a wretched fate to bear,
This constant need to wallow in despair,
You fret about the future and its woes,
And like a snowball rolling through the snows,
The weight of wretchedness just grows and grows.

The list of things to fret about is endless,
So often too the hapless wight feels friendless,
To find himself on every side beset,
By a self-inflicted pile of debt,
Or an affliction more oppressive yet,
From which few these days are entirely free:
A marriage partner's infidelity.

Despair of sinking in the void,
Despair of being unemployed,
Fear of sickness and of death,
Misery is the shibboleth,
And when all is undergone,
The misery goes on and on.

Now no one ever need despair at all,
We have a God of love on whom to call,
Christ Jesus is His name, our Burden-bearer,
And, pre-eminently, He is a carer;
He cares about the anguish of our hearts,
And willingly His soothing balm imparts,
Call on this Jesus in your hours of pain,
Nor dare His glorious friendship to disdain,
He has solutions ample and to spare,
To dissipate the worst case of despair.

Derek Sones

I Have Learned ...

That life moves in mysterious ways
That night is dark and light are the days
That we all suffer some kind of pain
Some days are sunny whilst others just rain
That good friends are there in times of need
Regardless of their colour or creed

Throughout the exciting journey of life
Some days can be filled with trouble and strife
Many events that happen can be put down to fate
So many people to meet to either love or hate

Not all life's events are given a reason or rhyme
They are not dictated by any season or time
Whatever life throws at you, you can always be sure
That some of these things leave us wanting more

But one thing is for sure, the *more* I have learned
The *less* I understand.

Karen Lewis

30th January

Believe In Yourself

Judge not yourself through hurt and pain,
For you are special and you are sane.
Hold on to your dreams, try not to cry,
Live not in despair by questioning why.

Live not in the past and leave it behind,
There are so many answers you will never find.
Be true to yourself, you're only one being,
If you wear a mask, you're hidden from seeing.

Don't be a pawn in the chess game they play,
Use all of your pieces, ignore what they say.
For when they say 'check' it's only your bait,
With success and happiness, you have 'check-mate'.

Let the head rule the heart, the tears will not flow,
When the sun is shining your shadow will grow.
Your lesson was learnt, there's no denial,
There are many that love you, be strong and *smile!*

Anthay

A Spiritual Cloak Of Love

I've made you a cloak to protect you
and keep you safe from harm
and although you cannot see it
I know it will keep you warm

For the threads that were used to make it
came from the spirit world above
each tiny intricate stitch that's in it
is a caring stitch of love

It radiates a feeling of peace
something that money cannot buy
it's warmer than the hottest fire
you have ever sat beside

It will add warmth to the heart that is crying
when feeling lost or alone
It will be your soothing comforter
and bring you peace within your soul

Don't worry when things beguile you
or when everything seems to be going wrong
the angels will place the cloak around you
helping to make your 'spirit' strong

Lilian Pickford-Miller

Smile!

A smile is so important
And often underrated
But a smile at another
Is soon reciprocated

A smile is infectious
So wear one on your face
And maybe this will help to make
The world a better place

Stein Dunne

Jesus Is Alive

Be true to Jesus
He is the one that saves us

Like the ocean wave
Jesus will bring life from the grave

Praise the Lord
Praise the Lord

Beauty is all around
Calling us
To the holy ground

Jesus is alive
He is coming back
To save us
Jesus is alive

Thank You Jesus
Thank You Jesus
Thank You Jesus.

Kenneth Mood

Peace

The peace beyond all understanding
So difficult to discover in our troubled world,
Sought nations wide by billions of folk
This elusive emotion, that many seek to find
This perfect peace, perfection
Found within our own hearts and mind
For those who truly find this golden gem
Gain inner riches far beyond material gain.

Duncan Robson

2nd February

An Invitation To The Lakes

What a beautiful sight, a joy to my eyes
Like a picture of artists renowned
The greens and the blues of varying hues
The sparkle of sun all around

The privilege, the pleasure
I have been given today
Will stay in my mind, that is true
The welcome given, the sharing of time
Happened only because of you

My mind is full of the beauty
I have seen
Each picture indelibly placed
So that when I am back home
Sitting alone
Those memories will never fade

Molly Ann Kean

3rd February

How Big Is Your Heart?

(To Pam, thanks for your love and support)

How big is your heart?
How wide is your resolve?
Have you scope ... dare you hope
That world peace can evolve?

Have you time for the beggar?
Have you patience for the old?
Is there respect for old enemies coming in from the cold?
Are you open and perhaps tolerant for another's point of view?
Is there a second in your busy life to say, 'What can I do?'

Would you expect nothing more if the roles were in reverse
And you faced a sad future like a victim of a curse?
Could you welcome a Samaritan, a Humanitarian or a neighbour just next door
With a tiny spark of human love that could make your spirits soar?

When you stared into a dark pit and despaired of finding love
Would you be glad of a helping hand to lift you up above?
I'm sure that now the answer has to be a yes
For we're put in this world to help those in distress
So make this a special year when goodness can really start
And I'll ask you once again my friend, just *how big is your heart?*

John Davies

Love Grows

Love grows
Love sustains
Love withers
Love dies
Life withers
Life dies
Where is love now?
Hope lives
Hope sustains
Hope does not wither
Hope loves life
Life, hope, love
Will come again

And it will.

Maggie Dennis

4th February

Climbing The Mountain Of Life

Some mountains are high and magnificent. Some are low
Why do people climb mountains? Because they are there
Some are easy to climb - just green slopes
Others have rocks to climb over or pass by
All climbers of mountains need the help of a guide
To lead them and find the best way
Sometimes the path is snow-covered or covered with a strange weed
Sometimes there are crevices or sharp stones to avoid
At all times a guide is needed to guide us
To keep on the path and not stray from it
Up and up the mountain the climbers go
Looking around at the beauty seen on the way
Sometimes a bird, some flowers, a cloud or another mountain
On some mountains several people climb together
On others, just one on the rope
To climb is like our journey on Earth
Sometimes things go well, sometimes there's danger
Pitfalls and the going is tough
We need our heavenly guide with us
All the way to gently direct us
Life is like a mountain we climb each day
Until we reach the summit and our heavenly home
Where we are welcomed by our Lord.

Jean Martin-Doyle

True Love

My eyes transfixed on your potent stare
Worldly troubles just fly on by
My thoughts contemplate little else
So mesmerised by your beauty
My inner feelings for you transparent
My face transmitting unequivocal joy
To live without you is unthinkable
How did I manage it before?
As the sun goes down on yet another day
I know I should reflect
Two kindred spirits on their own
But with each other evermore.

John Warren

5th February

I've Got You

All through the day
To You God ...
I can chatter away
Knowing You won't mind
As You are loving and kind
My best friend and dad
I could ever have,
Whatever I do
I'll keep close to You
That's where I want to stay
By Your side every day.
I've got You to hold me tight
And make things right
I know for me You love and care
And will always be there
I couldn't want for more
You are the reason I'm living for.
When Earthly people let me down
You will always be around
Me You will take care of
I've got You God ...

Lindy Roberts

My Love

Your smile means so much to me
More than you'll ever know,
And every time we meet my love
I mean to tell you so.

I'm not a man of many words
But I would like to say
Please stay with me forever
Forever and a day.

And if someday we should ever part
And this love of ours would end,
My heart would be forever broken
And never more would mend.

So let us walk together as one
So I can call you mine,
And stay with me for evermore
Until the end of time.

Bob Lowe

Visions Of Hope

Flowers on the window sill
Snowflakes on the trees
A fire burning quietly
Warmth is what you see
A petal falling softly
A tear on your cheek
The wind whistles outside
As you gently speak
A rose withered away
A candle long burnt out
Lacy curtains hanging
Away from the ice which melts
A churning in your stomach
Darkness all around
Although the stars shine brightly
Sadness has you bound
Dream of another tomorrow
But sense a dulling ache
Tension is created
But silence is all you make
Howling of the wolves proceed
A glimpse of the moon
The fire flickers in your eyes
Daylight will bring hope soon.

Michelle Harvey

8th February

Winter Days

In the dreary winter days
I find pleasure in many ways
The lovely colours in the sky
As the day says goodbye
In the garden too I find
Berries bright of every kind
Food for the birds
In winter days
Pleasing in so many ways

I Millington

Untitled

On a cold winter's day,
Looking across a wide-open bay,
Birds in flight
Can be such a wonderful sight.
Watching a candle burn in the light,
Wishing with all your might.
Days go slow
Waiting for the snow,
Or just for spring to grow.
My life is just a slow train crawling up a hill,
Like the sails on a windmill.
Days when you can't find,
When losing your mind.
Silence is deafening.
Your memories you are defending,
Or longing for a friend,
On a cold winter's day.

Cath Powell

Weather Or Not

Though the weather is grey,
You'll find I feel great,
I really don't know how I entered this state.
It's freezing outside, everyone has a hat on,
A chill in the air,
Yet it's warmth that I'm sat on.
There's rain on the windows,
Dark clouds in the sky,
And no explanation for feeling so high.
Others look drained,
I used to be one of those,
From Monday to Monday,
My mind a lake that had froze.
Now my body feels different,
My mind rearranged,
It's equally pleasant and equally strange.
One day you will feel how I'm feeling now,
Unsure when you'll get there, so hold on for now.
And though the report says, 'Rain for tomorrow',
Never confuse bad weather with sorrow.

Craig Brown

Grey And Cold

The days are grey and cold
There is snow on the way we are told
It may be white over with frost in the morning
So take care and take heed of the warning.

Go out, try not to slip or fall down
As this will cause you to frown
If you fall, try to land on your bum
So as not to feel too numb.

Then you will not feel so sore
That is what your bum is for
Try not to look around
As someone will spot you, you'll be bound.

So let's hope for the snow
So we at least know
To stop inside and be warm
And then you will not come to any harm.

Garry Bedford

11th February

One Cloud Is Mine

No amount of 'I'm sorry' will ever ease the pain
No amount of time will ever replace his name.
There's an empty space in our double bed
And the nights just get longer as the days stretch ahead.
It seems pointless somehow, to make pots of tea
When there's no one to share, there is only me.
But I look through the photos and twist my gold band,
And think of the days when we travelled the land.
We laughed and we cuddled, we shouted and kissed
I swallow a lump, you are 'so very' missed.
But I have to be strong as I look at my bump
And remember the joy as we climbed 'the mump'.
Your child will be born, conceived out of love
And I know you will watch from your cloud high above.

Janice Melmoth

Clouds

Look at the clouds,
Fluffy shapes in the sky.
They'll turn into pictures,
If you give it a try.
They may form a duck,
A cow or a horse.
But they're really just clouds,
Drifting by on their course.

Jay Berkowitz

Pause

How quick the hours of the day,
some time lingering on
what we need to say.
In sharing moments,
holding precious,
tender expression,
that heals with understanding
and brings the calm
light shining through,
guiding once more
to centre, Lord, on You.

A J Brooking

13th February

Continue Ye In My Love

We took a walk through some woods one Sunday
And the scene set off another memory
Of where she had once walked before.
Trees triggered memories, leaves left lingering thoughts.
She shared her story of the sun.

She knew nothing of the journey before it began.
The sun was peeping through the branches
Of the trees that sheltered and protected her.
Refreshing raindrops quenched her thirst.
'And ye shall find rest unto your souls
For My yoke is easy and My burden is light'.
But then she tripped and fell.

There's a different perspective from the ground.
The sun still shone above but she could not see beyond.
The trees became oppressive and suffocating
And raindrops fell like tears.
'Greater love hath no man than this,
That a man lay down his life for his friends'.
But she said He did not die for her.

In a moment of chance she looked up and saw
The sun lighting the way to beckon her to safety.
The trees supported her, helping her to her feet
As she walked, following the river of truth and freedom.
'As the Maker hath loved me, so I have loved you:
Continue ye in My love,' He said.
She believed with all her heart.

Tessa Jane Lee

14th February

The Parting Valentine

You have left this life my darling
Leaving sadness in my heart
God's will and recent calling
Decided we must part
My life ahead without you
Will be such a painful test
Until once more we meet again
In God's land of peaceful rest
Until that day, my darling
Your memory is my light
To help me through the remaining years
Of my long and lonely nights
The years we had together
Though joyful, now seem brief
For your light extinguished from my life
There seems no bright relief
Here in St Swithin's churchyard
Close to your memory stone
A rose to spread its dewdrops
My tears for you alone
Rest in peace my darling
For you, my saddened heart does pine
As in life may you stay forever
My only Valentine

E L Hannam

14th February

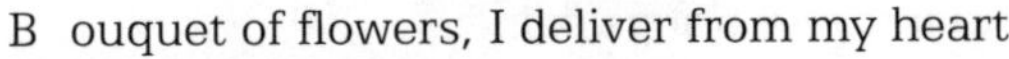

B ouquet of flowers, I deliver from my heart
E ach petal represents my love waiting to start

M ore colourful than a field of flowers in blossom
Y ou'll marvel at the fragrance, spinning round the room

V ery devoted to bring on air of beauty
A rranged only for you, you'll like the scenery
L ove the picture; take hold of it in your arms
E scape from the darkness enjoy the tender charms
N eeds to be fed and watered with your loving care
T reat in such a way, demands your dynamic flair
I t will live forever, accept invitation
N o doubt about feelings waits investigation
E asy let it flow, our love will constantly grow

John Neal

15th February

Why Worry?

Worrying is harmful, worrying brings pain
Not only that, worrying drives you insane
Worrying drives you crazy, you know that's true
So if you are a worrier here's what to do

Don't you worry, don't you fret
Don't worry about your health
Don't worry about your debt
Don't worry about your housework
When your children want to play
Don't worry about your future
Just live for today

Just live for today and have some fun
Just live for today and the war will be won
Just live for today and you will see
A happier you - worry free.

Elaine Phillips

No More Tears

(For Frank, Kevin and Victoria for their loving support)

Why are you crying?
A tiny droplet all moist and clear

Lift your head and wipe your eyes
And brush away your trickling tear

Like the stars that spear the darkest sky
Your sadness cannot mask

The brightness shining out when head held high
And in the sunny warmth to bask

Ponder your unhappy gaze
Sour thought through endless days

Banish quickly all the spite
Lift your mood from dark to light

Keep your thoughts and cast the doubt
When the time is right you'll shout

I'm not crying any longer
My eyes are dry, I'm growing stronger.

Shirley Perkins

16th February

The Wonder Of Acceptance ...

Peace can never be found,
If it's not alive in your heart,
Once you find it you should keep it,
And never allow it to depart.

If worries build up inside you,
Until you feel they're too much,
Let them go within the safety,
Of a loved one's tender touch.

If pain finds a way in,
Then refuses to leave,
There's one small trick,
You can keep up your sleeve.

Begin to understand what hurts,
And accept why it's there,
Have faith things can get better,
And never stop believing that people do care!

Louise Pamela Webster

16th February

He Is Always There For Us

Last night I dreamt I was trying
To find my way home,
I was on a hill,
And I had no idea how I got there.
I tried to find a way of getting down,
But I couldn't,
There were no shortcuts, no path,
Not even a paw or footprint.

It began to get dark,
I started feeling quite scared,
The first trickle of tears ran down my face.
I dug deep in my pockets,
Found a crumpled tissue,
Wiped the tears away
And told myself I had to be strong,
So I started to pray.

Suddenly out of the darkness,
Shone a bright light,
And someone called out my name.
The voice was gentle, like that of a friend,
I looked up and to my amazement
Was an outstretched hand.
I held it and it led me right back to my door.

I knew then God had answered my prayer,
And even though I was on my own,
I was not alone,
Because He is always with us,
Especially in difficult times.

Pauline E Reynolds

Horizons

To far horizons youthful eyes are drawn,
Enticing prospects spread along the way.
New goals to strive for as new hopes are born,
A shining future gilding present day.

Both time and distance shrink as years pass by,
Compelling duties claim each vacant space,
No longer flights of fancy mount so high,
And pleasures wear a simple homely face.

Age calls for patience to accept constraint,
To focus on horizons within reach.
As limbs grow feeble, sight and hearing faint,
How precious are good friends and thought and speech!

For joys of life can never quite be over
While there is time to watch bees in the clover.

V E Godfrey

Lawnmower Hibernation

I clean it down and put it in the shed
Though it gets later every year
And it could be out in March!

For now we're left with leaves to seep,
Soil to turn, rubbish to burn!
Making sure our spiky garden friend
Hasn't made his home among.

The birds visit more, and we see them fully clothed.
Not long ago, they brought young,
Lining up unsteadily on garden fence
To be fed! Tatty and exhausted by hungry mouths to feed.

The robin shares some time with me
As I throw him a worm.
Not tame! Just a free meal ticket
But I marvel all the same.

The frost and snow arrive
I walk deserted fields
Seeing signs of spring in mid winter.
Buds, shoots, new leaves out too soon.

Smell of wet earth, frosted air assails my nostrils ...
And I breathe a cloud of white steam!
Yes, I like winter
When the lawnmower goes into hibernation.

I can get my senses finely tuned
And looking to the wonderful starry sky,
Navigate myself through another year.

E Osmond

18th February

For A Troubled Friend

Can't take any more?
Then don't.
Submit to God.
Let Him carry you for a while,
Just till you're stronger.

Calm your troubled mind.
Don't chase agitated thoughts,
Round maniacal merry-go-rounds.
Don't forcibly try to still them,
Just let them be.

Inattention will eject them,
Peace will reign once more.
Stronger you will rebuild your life.
Remember life is good,
A gift from God.

Learn to forgive.
Yourself as well as others.
We all share the human condition,
Subject to the same weaknesses,
But also capable of greatness.

Nurture your friendships.
They are more precious than gold.
Hold fast to family, they are home,
Not bricks and furniture.

Be kind to yourself.
You have a unique place in time and space.
A purpose only you can fulfil.
Not yours to know how or why till time is done.
Be happy, that is success.

Teresa Garfield

19th February

The Art Of Meditation

When I awoke, the dream was vivid in my mind,
I felt happy, inspired, all difficulties
Were resolved, relationships changed from passion to
Purity, I was filled with joy. After years of
Searching I knew the answer, now so apparent,
After going full-circle I was back at the
Beginning, to start once again in innocence,
Without guilt, remorse, doubt. Faith restored,
All desire and attachment ceased, only object
Remained, the essence, not the false created by
The senses, delusions, rich imagination.
With revelation came peace which hitherto
Had eluded me. By concentration, effort,
The mind loses itself in truth, beyond desire.
By meditation: on the Earth, air, water, wind,
Sun, moon and stars, the wise, beautiful, virtuous,
On any form, male or female, on any god
That you love, any form as seen in a mirror,
The form does not matter, it is the power of
Meditation that counts. When mind's activity
Is controlled, illumination results. When mind
Refuses to be swayed, when by concentration
Loses itself in the true sense of being,
The subject, the object, the instrument become one.

Betty Mealand

Try Again

Bring down the walls of hurt and pain
And have the faith you'll love again
It's hard to mend a break in the heart
When you feel your world's been torn apart.

You thought the words he said were true
And life was being so good to you
With all the hurt and all the lies
A beautiful heart withers and dies.

Have the strength to start again
Begin to heal all the pain
Build up the trust, the faith, the hope
Believe in yourself, you'll start to cope.

The crying stops, you start to mend
You feel the love your guardians send
Trust and support from friends so dear
Warms your heart, melts the fear.

Positive thoughts along the way
Will lighten the load, brighten the day
Life goes on, no second best
New love appears, you've passed the test.

Believe the words, how good they feel
And this is love, love so real
No fear, no pain, no hurt, no doubt
This is what love is all about.

Carol Bosisto

21st February

A Love Song For The Earth

With my heart beating in rare February sun
I feel ecstatic pulsating love for this bed of earth
and hawks crying heavenward from their open beaks
the newly-dug rabbit hole in the pale red dirt
light gleaming on a winding ribbon of road
the tentative buds of daffodils waiting to open
pheasants wandering through the frosted grass
this diorama built around my doorstep, my place

My heart chokes when the plenty seeps in,
the sun like a grandfather, a golden armchair
surrounded by cold layers of air
trees' arms reaching overhead
they way the owls call and baby rabbits fall
softly out of the hedge

There is a river mist and a woodpecker
tattooing by the stream
a blackbird coming for seed
and the wren whose stub of a tail flicks
like a tiny mouse on the run

Something in the atmosphere holds it
together, as though a song was being written
in that moment and the notes were breaking
into heartbeats and rhythms that would spread
down to the worms beneath and the clouds overhead
and right into the tree trunks and the rocks and the sheep;
as though hearing and watching the music
was the heaven of life

Karen Eberhardt-Shelton

Corinthians

The eloquence of angels, without charity
Is but the strident banging of a gong.
The gifts of faith and reason, lacking clarity
Do little to release the world from wrong.
The sacrifice of wealth to feed the poor
Must surely be inspired by love, by charity;
To give one's life, refusing to ignore
The Third World's gasping, desperate disparity.
Patience, kindness, modesty, contentment,
Warm compassion are the signs of charity,
Clear of lies and pride and just resentment,
Friendship melting any insularity.
Love is paramount and, fast entwined
With faith and hope, embraces all mankind.

Vaughan Stone

One

In a one to one love relationship
There is no dictatorship
Just because you've done one
Doesn't mean you are one.
The name Dad follows on
Because you're my dad; my one,
I'm travelling light because of one
You are the way; and my respected one.

Vera Collins

23rd February

Sky Art

Billowing, scudding, cumulus clouds,
Starkly white against azure blue,
A continuous, flowing, sculptured mass
Allowing unrestrained imaginings.
Metamorphosing, transmuting freely
An emancipated, untrammelled nebulosity
Careless of the machinations of Man.

Rose-Mary Gower

24th February

Tender Draws The Night

Tender draws the night
and with its slow caress,
puts abed the sun.
The silence ...
bringing peace that strokes the land,
follows like a blanket,
softly drawn.
And as the gilding of the heavens
reveals a beauty
deeper still than day,
look now
... and see eternity.
For where in this God-given universe,
... in this blue-sceptred isle
that roams the universe,
can beauty such as this
compare with thee?

Stretch your mind far ...
... far into the distance,
and speak with stars
that blaze their pathway through the heavens.
Walking thro' time ...
feel the rhythm of the ages
pulse and grow within you.
The ebb,
the flow,
the spirit!
... of life.

Bob Tose

Day In Pithagori

Day in Pithagori
Looking out to sea
Bay where once was glory
Young man who was free

Pine trees so much cooler
Fig trees smell the shade
Never love my ruler
Never love persuade

Waves with all their fury
Thundering close by
Octaves sweet amore
Underneath the sky

Sea was getting calmer
Somewhere near the town
Letting down his armour
As the sun went down

Dolphins were appearing
Soaring each in turn
All the time surpassing
Sea began to churn

Near a wreck came gliding
Where the sun turns red
Dolphin's neck - boy hanging
Fair his bobbing head

Quick the young man running
Dolphins' final call
Music then was deafening
Gone amidst the squall

Tom Ritchie

26th February

Magnolias

Elegant, poised, graceful and bright,
Tender, yet strong, reaching to the light.
Standing tall, but able to bend,
Like stately magnolias - women of strength.

Silken-white blooms, can be damaged by frost,
Giving off fragrance, whatever the cost,
Creative, inspiring to great extent
Not strong women, but women of strength.

Cool, serene and dignified,
Resourceful, capable, would describe
The way they do their job with pride,
Hearts like steel, but soft inside.

An aura of beauty, when they stand alone,
Will blend with others, but thrive well on their own,
A perfume surrounds them, like buds bursting forth,
Positive women, women of worth.

Rooted in fertile soil so deep,
Feeding on nutrients, that will keep
Sending up shoots, giving new birth,
Women of strength, replenishing the Earth.

Ella Mae Agnew

The Visitor

I search with eager eyes, each bush and tree.
Hidden from me, he waits with hungry stare.
I know he's waiting eagerly for me,
Our tryst a daily secret we two share.

His wary, natural fear is his defence.
The clicking lock his signal to come near.
Hearing rustles, seeing movement I sense
Hunger drives away his natural fear.

I give him food he now has come to like
When insects shrink away from bitter cold,
And beak gets no reward for probing strike.
Some loyalty for feathered friends I hold.

Blackbirds, sparrows, robins, these at least
Gather for breakfast, watch, peck, and bring
Partners, all rivals, gather at my feast.
Respite from winter, build their strength for spring.

Janice Ginever

28th February

A Day By The Sea

The reflection of sun, a gentle breeze,
The softness of sand, that never fails to please,
The ripples on sea, the cry of the gull,
The molluscs that fix themselves firmly to hull,
The odd stranded crab, a starfish or two,
The foamy waves creeping towards me and to you,
The trawlers afar, with following birds,
The razorfish buried in the depths, unstirred,
The cracking of sail, the flag on the buoy,
The bucket and spade and occasional toy,
The parent with child, building castles galore,
With moat, tower and turrets, times 2, 3 or 4,
The stripes of the deckchairs, erected in error,
Which fluster, confuse and instil fear and terror,
The smell of the chips which accompany fish,
Served up in a nice polystyrene dish,
Which often will find their way into the sea,
And float away northwards, like rafts, after tea,
Then after time passes, the sun sets down low,
And bathers to B&Bs local, do go,
Then in comes the sea and swallows the beach,
And its damp little fingers, into crevices reach,
And out slip crustaceans, who don't feel the cold,
To wander the galleys of wrecks, young and old,
Then, in quiet of night, when the sky is quite pink,
You return to your real life, where this day makes you think,
Of the beauty of living in a world such as this,
Where the lips of the sea, gave your toes a cold kiss.

Hilary Ayling

1st March

A Reflection On The First Day Of March

Of March, 'tis
The very first day,
Its winds exhilarating
To lift the spirits
And blow our
Winter blues away.
March has come
As gloom dispels
And newborn lambs
Upon the hills
Do play.
Soon, in their profusion,
Yellow daffodils
In the breeze
Will sway.
God's bounty
Now in plenty,
As March has come
With brighter days,
To the Creator
Each songbird
Sings his song
Of praise.

Brigid Smith

Spring

Spring! Excitement, surprise and colour - spring!
A season of life, a most enjoyable thing!
Winter's past, bad weather's cast -
She's here, spring has come at last!

She skates over the beds dead and brown,
Wearing her majestic garb and windy crown.
She draws the snowdrops from earth's clutch
With her strong and steady magnetic touch

Daffodils, crocus, hyacinth blue,
A touch of green, a refreshing hue;
New colours, new songs and new air too;
Even the sky is a different blue!

Birds chant their songs, that all winter long
Have swelled in their throats to break into song.

Dorothy M Kemp

A Treasure Chest

God's promises are rich beyond measure.
When we open the bible of treasure
He tells us how we should live
Then shows how to forgive.
So dear God, when I look to you each day,
Help me walk on life's pathway
Then I may receive
The blessings, when I believe
Your goodness that dwells
Richly in my heart
To give me a brand new start.
Forgetting the past
And my burdens I can cast
A rainbow is in sight
So I can be happy and bright.

Caron P Simpson

2nd March

After The Blizzard

It was winter when he came
with his broken hurt to mend.

Like a sudden storm of snow,
quick to fall, covering slow.

The disbelief, just one night
life was normal, fun and bright,
home a haven of warm light.

Avalanche in morning gloom
shattered all within that room,
portrait of the bride and groom

smashed pieces of broken ice,
betrayed by lover's secret vice,
mocked the wedding dress and rice.

Questioning words on frozen lips,
fearful, chosen phrasing slips
into frosty, legal scripts.

Heart, a fire of scorching oil,
blistering downpour sears soil,
scatters slicing sleet, to foil

unanswered doubts arise,
'What did I do wrong?' he cries.
Voice dissolved in leaden skies.

Spring has thawed, her softening rain
renews green shoots - life grows again.

New-found soulmate lifts the pain,
heals his heart - with love unchained.

Leigh Crighton

Night And Day

The fingers of night pluck the sun from the sky,
The birds fly home to their nests on high,
The cows and the sheep are all asleep,
And lie safe and warm until morning is nigh.

The stars in the sky are the eyes of the night,
The moon hangs low with her silvery light,
The babes in their beds rest their sleepy heads,
To wake with a smile when the sun shines bright.

The night is over, the day has begun,
The birds and the beasts fly high and have fun,
The children play in the warmth of the day,
And all is at peace till the night steals the sun!

Frances Walker

4th March

Marguerite

You touched the lives of all who knew you,
our grief and sense of loss are hard to bear,
we are the poorer now that you have left us,
we counted on your always being there.

The heavens are the brighter for your passing,
a new star has appeared which glows with light,
much as your loving spirit shone in life,
so it will spread its rays throughout the night.

Your legacy lives on and this will guide us,
we'll always keep your memory alive,
our thoughts of you are filled with joy and laughter,
through you we'll grow and surely will survive.

Angela R Davies

The Passage Of Life

The apparitions on the mountain of hope
Dispel notions of an eternity of nothing
With time in clandestine meetings of renewal
As nature responds to a changing world
Of sin and heartfelt tragedy
But the thousand sorrows
Are complemented by a thousand tomorrows
As the hourglass of destiny
Spins every grain of sand
Marking a new soul in transition
From this world
To the next astral plain
As the axis of heavenly symmetry
Is tilted towards forgiveness
In the fullness of life
And the immortality of death.

Finnan Boyle

Bluebells In The Meadow

I walked along the Old Vicarage Road and up the steepened hill
Which bent and increased with my every stride.
The trees arched their covered green arms across the road
And through the leaves I can see dancing light.
Warm and bright, shimmering speckles of daydreams and
Swirling leaves making the tunnel seem brief.

A brisk wind whispers around me, 'Are we really quite alone?' but ...
Blackbirds forage for worms then dance and skip into hedgerows
Pruned where cattle sit in magnificent meadows,
Lazily swooning, nodding heads and their swiping tails.

'Quietly'
I reach the distance I want to be, 'the second seat' and rest awhile to catch my breath.
Then stroll dreamily down the hill to see bluebells in the meadow
Stretching wide and free, then glancing between the trees,
This small town sits at a different angle - that I have ever seen
Which makes me wonder, 'When do we ever live a life as calm
And free as this moment?'

Carole Morris

Mother's Love

Our mother, our mummy, our mum,
A treasure to talk to, for those who have one,
Someone special in our lives, whose need
Is constant, compassionate, understanding, a lead.

A smile that's a greeting, lovely to see,
Sharing her life, as a golden key,
A key that unlocks sound advice,
Offered diplomatically, honestly, very precise.

Hands so comforting, a reassuring strength,
Holding as an anchor, her essence, her scent.
Around the table, discussions as friends,
Whatever topic, free spirit, one could depend.

Memories, when the hands of time have answered *God's* call,
Remembered as always, loved by us all.
So many things, we find are still here,
Reminding us all, as we brush away a tear.

Lorna Tippett

Living Inspiration

(Respectfully dedicated to my most affectionate mother, 'Merna'.
Thank you very much, Mam, for everything that you have ever done for me throughout my life to date - with deeply heartfelt gratitude - from Michael, himself)

Constant awareness of the truly timeless pace itself
does indeed fully ferment the ageless quest of
priceless rancour within the depth of
obviously contestable comeliness,
to justify exactly the strictly honourable progress
of the rapidly flowing waters.

Then in purely graphic motion to
end this yearly cycle with the real abundance of
those strongly solidified fortifications to
empower the collective essence of the
rotating planet Earth itself in all due time.

Michael Denholme Hortus Stalker

Laughter

The hawthorn's clowning in hedgerows,
The days are growing fat,
Primroses cartwheel along the lanes
And a pale moons doffs
Its hat
At winter trees.

Rachel Leivers

8th March

Birth Day Of The Earth

It is the birth day of the Earth
On the 8th of March
Is it in your calendar
Or are you at a party on the moon away so far?

It is the birth day of the Earth
Yet only the Chinese can see
Because it means a lot to them
More than it means to you and me.

It is the birth day of the Earth
Yet its true age no one knows
How much longer can it keep going?
Yet no slowing down, it never shows.

Keith L Powell

8th March

Everything In Thee

Give me the grace O Lord:
In ev'ry need in Thee to trust
At ev'ry turn Thy will to seek
By ev'ry way Thy name to bless.

Benjamin Takavarasha

9th March

Spirit Of Spring Song

Oh the sun has come again,
warm and inviting!

So many days have passed,
the sun masked by grey skies,
clouds painting a sombre canvas,
framed with cold,
now and then a snow flurry
to brighten the winter steel.

But the sun has come again,
warm and inviting!

All is joyous as I turn my face to the sun.
I feel the welcome rays
caressing my face and hair.

Now flowers will make gay,
opening from buds,
vivid colours will glow.
Blossom will drape the stark bough,
in blankets of pink and white delight.

Oh everything is wonderful in our world!
The sun has come again,
warm and inviting.

Carol Ann Darling

The Beauty Of A Tree

Wandering over the hills and thro' vales,
Enjoying the scenery of the Yorkshire Dales,
Each time rapt with admiration, roaming free,
I swear I have seen nothing so perfect as a tree,
Stately, upright, dignified, glorious, crooked, bent,
Soldiering on, regardless, though storms may rent
Her magnificence, her pride rudely shattered,
Presenting her seared trunk, her soul battered,
She rises again, sends out a shoot,
Seeking sun and rain, to take root.

In gentle breezes, shimmering branches dance,
Capturing the eye with more than one glance
And it seems God speaks His creation's praise,
His most beauteous works to outlive my days
On this Earth, where His wondrous plants grow,
Displaying lofty elegance thro' nature's flow,
To replenish bright greenery for our delight,
Releasing life-giving gases into the night,
She proudly carries out her task
'Neath branches so shady, to bask!

Whole forests of trees bring such pleasure,
Many joyful moments beyond all measure,
When we simply slow down to drink in beauty,
To rest now and then, our bounden duty
To admire God's handiwork, His works of art
Steadying our lives, graciously play their part,
Seed-bearers, fruit-givers, wood-bearing trees,
Are there to help souls, to bring great ease.
Most majestic objects in this life -
Trees, of such beauty, ease our strife.

Julia Eva Yeardye

Lifted

My spirit has lifted
With the dawning
Of a new day
With daffodils blooming
Bright yellow that
Proudly stand.
For a while
My soul was lost
To the rush of life
To make a name and
Fight for fame.
The simplicity of beauty
Found me
The toil of life
Forced me behind
A dark cloud.
Now I can shine
Once more
With daffodils blooming
To a bright new day.

Penny Kirby

11th March

Mother's Love

When I'm lying down in bed
Things come to me which my mother said
And I praise the God above
For my mother and her love.

It is easy now to see
What my mother meant to me
And I have two children dear
Who are glad that I am here.

May I show her selfless care
Acts of giving anywhere
May her thoughtfulness remain
So that I can do the same.

Robert S Dell

11th March

The Smallest Little Bird Survives

Chirp, warble and peep in my ear,
The little bird sings, his message is clear.
He tells me the smallest birds of them all,
Have the loudest shrieks and shrills for their call.
He proudly boasts his position and fame,
Smallest of all yet part of the game.
Chirping and peeping and shrilling away,
Warbling and shrieking till night takes the day.
A tiny soul with a voice so loud,
Determined, fierce, strong and proud.
He knows his position, he knows his place,
His song, joyful, from a blissful face.

Tom Fox

12th March

Angel's Smile

Hidden smile, whispering word
To be seen, seldom heard
From a child pulled side to side
Stuck between anger and pride

Behind the doors of plastic love
Tears unseen a heart to shove
To know the pain planted deep
Honesty, truth my heart can sleep

Moving on to teenage blues
With brittle heart, confidence bruised
Thumping memories scream and shout
Legs like jelly, passing out

From angry waves to ripple of calm
A kiss of comfort, compatible charm
To have found the truth a heart to rest
Happiness, strength found my quest

With shining armour a beautiful man
The angel's smile I know is Nan
A mind clear, a heart to rest
From above, my soul now blessed.

R S Wayne Hughes

13th March

It's Spring

Again Mother Nature begins to rise
Wiping away winter from her eyes,
She stretches and blows the frost away
Getting ready to welcome a new spring day.

She warms the Earth so the flowers will grow
They've been asleep all winter protected from snow,
Snowdrops and crocus are the first to peep
From the ground so snug and deep,

Daffs and tulips are the next to come
Shimmering brightly in the springtime sun,
A carpet of colour to catch your eye
From the purple and yellow to the blue of the sky.

She beckons the birds to spread the news
It's time to shake off those winter blues,
Sing your song loud and clear
Tell everyone that spring is here.

Margaret Anne Hedley

Bright Side

A new breath is my token
As my eyes do open
Silent birds have spoken
Clouded skies to be broken
For rays of warm light brighten
Our Mother Earth is awoken
So time brings life to motion
Step forward to drink thy potion
Positive energies colour our lotion
Rainbows diving from the ocean
Stand tall and touch this horizon
Watch, for all thy doors will open
Step forward, see your stars brighten
Smell these flowers of emotion
For a new day is our notion.

Grant Kinnaird

15th March

Looking Back

Upon reflections every day,
I think of things that passed my way,
Of how the good things made me glad,
And not so good ones made me sad,
Looking way back over years,
Some brought gladness, others tears,
All we can do is hope and pray
This year some good will come our way.

Betty Mason

Fallen Flower

So young, she drooped and fell
And kissed the stony path
My golden daffodil of spring;
O that I'd bound her stem
To stand erect
My lovely maiden flower!
Now not to meet again
'Til next spring's joyous hour.

Michael Rowson

17th March

One Little Word

Repeat this little word over and over in your head
Repeat it when you wake and before you go to bed

Share it with your family and share it with your friends
Share it all your life from beginning to the end

Let it show through all your actions, today and every day
Let it be your guiding light pointing out the way

It may be just a little word, it may be very small
But when you let *joy* in your life you won't look back at all.

Denise Watson

18th March

I Started To Rebuild My Faith

I used to think, when I was young,
That when you died, your world was 'done'.
I used to wonder, think and cry,
I asked why God made people die.
I asked why He took them away,
My friends and family, why couldn't they stay?
No one explained why they had to leave,
I thought God was cruel, I refused to believe.

But something told me it was not black and white,
And I started to think, (in the dark of the night),
That maybe death wasn't the end of it all,
Was it something to do with God and His call?
I realised that there was more after life,
To relieve us of Earth's pain and its strife.
I didn't know where, but now I was sure
That there really must be something more.

After several thoughtful days and many long nights,
I'd decided that I must be right.
I thought when we died, God made us safe,
And I started to rebuild my faith.
I realised that death wasn't so bad,
So when loved ones were gone I tried not to be sad.
It seemed to me that death was relief,
And that God didn't mean to cause such grief.

Now, stronger than ever, I feel the same,
And no longer hold my God to blame.
I see that life goes beyond the grave,
That we go to Heaven and really, are saved.

Leanne Mizen

Moo

Don't eat me Mister, Mister Glum,
For I've a father and a mum.
I'd like to graze, in lofty fields,
Then lock'd in sheds and fed on pills.
I'd like to live till I am old,
Impossible, this I am told.
I'll probably end up on your plate
Then my requests will be too late.
Please treat me well, as I would you
For the hand that taketh me, one day will take you!

L Goldsmith

A Blessing

May the morning sun
shower soft petals on your face.
May the gentle rain
fall softly on your days
and speak to you of spring.
May your mind and soul
be filled with God's light and grace
and through loving kindness,
may your heart grow strong in love
and beat with its own special song.

Let us receive each day with the gratitude and tenderness
of a mother receiving her newborn child.
Let us ponder and accept the blessing of each new day
with all of its seasons.
Give your blessing to others, careful to leave them better
than when you found them;
treating each person with the reverence you would give
one of nature's most beautiful spaces.
Let each person become that sacred space,
a place to stand before in awe and wonder.

Anne-Marie Ryan-Tucker

21st March

God's Inspiration

You give me the freshness
Of the cool, clear, morning air,
The pale blue sky above me,
And the rising sun framed there.

You give me the promise
Of a new day's early light,
The glimmer of the golden sun,
Shining on all in sight.

You give me the bright hope,
That the washed, clean daylight brings,
When all of Nature, in harmony,
Raises its voice and sings.

You give me the newness
Of your natural, living earth,
And my heart's full of inspiration,
At each welcome morning's birth.

Lorna Lea

22nd March

Thanks

Well, you are all so special
And I guess I am as well
I'm a very special person
With a story now to tell

I know you might have worried
Just like my mum and dad
But you see I'm a little fighter
Things really weren't that bad

I suppose if I was honest
I was just a little scared
But I was in the many prayers
Of everyone who cared

Everyone was worried
But they didn't need to be
Because you were there to give me hope
And take good care of me

I know you have a hard job
And that you work through night and day
Just to help people like me
And get us on our way

So, I really want to thank you
But I just don't know where to start
You see you gave me another chance
The day you fixed my heart.

Kim Mehaffy

22nd March

A Small Boy

They were thrilled by His teaching
They experienced His healing
He was different.
His dark, penetrating eyes reflected love
They saw into your inner being
Nothing could lie hidden
They could not have enough of the teacher
The carpenter from Galilee.
Sat on the hillside
Five thousand or more, listening.
Time goes, still they do not move.
'Give them food,' He says
'We have nothing,' His disciples reply.
A small boy, moved by those eyes,
Offers his picnic
Five loaves, two fish
What good will they be?
In the hands of the teacher
In the blessings He gives
Over bread and fish
Wonder of wonders
Five thousand are fed.

Shirley Ludlow

23rd March

Pennies For My Thoughts

Oh how I wish, if that
was at all possible,
to turn the clock back
to the Britain of the 50s
and recount those enchanted
years of not so long ago,
when one ...
- was proud of his name
- could safely walk the streets
- showed respect to others
- could go on a bus for 3 pence
and to the flicks for a bob
- could have a meal
at the Lyon's corner house
for 2 and 6 pence.

Alas today, in the name of progress
and commercialisation, all that
Britain stood for then has gone
forever, never to return.
Perhaps that is why today,
droves of people on their retirement
leave Britain for 'greener pastures' abroad
where they think life would be kinder
and similar to the one, they were used to.

As for me, I would always choose
the uncomplicated life of the 50s.

P P Christodoulides

24th March

Hope to begin
Hope to be free
Hope to hear good news
Hope to brighten your day
Hope to spread some happiness
Hope to bring endless joy
Hope to celebrate
Hope to grow in faith
Hope to be successful
Hope to give thanks
Hope for some caring
Hope for some love
Hope for some peace
Hope for some kindness
Hope for a special wish
Hope for something that's possible
Hope for happiness today and always
Hope for the future
Hope is for justice
Hope is for ordinary people
Hope is everything
Hope is to hold dear
Hope is truly inspiring
Hope is the feeling of trust
Hope is promising
Hope gives us fulfilment
Hope gives us meaning
Hope gives us life
Hope God will be your guide
Hope God will stay by your side.

Rita Scott

24th March

I Want To Be A Tree

Oh, how simple life would be,
If I were not a person, but a humble tree,
I'd stand proud and majestic, without a care,
No need for clothes or worry about bad hair.
No cooking, washing or cleaning would I do,
I'd gaze at a sky of cornflower blue.
No screaming children causing a riot,
Just gentle calm, peace and quiet.

But what about birds? In my branches they'd nest,
From their constant chattering there'd be no rest.
Then there are squirrels that scrabble and scratch,
And a little later the eggs will hatch.
Hundreds of babies, their beaks open wide,
Waiting for Mum to pop food inside.
Hoards of insects and woodpeckers pecking,
And what if, *gulp*, I were chopped down for decking?

Autumn winds will whistle and whip,
From delicate branches, my leaves they strip.
In the winter cold, I am bare and forlorn,
No woolly sweaters to keep me warm.
It's a long time until spring and warmer weather,
I'm frozen and miserable, at the end of my tether.
So it's really quite stressful, the life of a tree,
I think on reflection, I'd much rather be me.

Louise Wheeler

25th March

When Life Gets To Me

I should be thankful and always count my many blessings
I try but don't always succeed and instead I shout
I rant, I rave about life being so unfair
And how fate has singled me, and only me, out.

Life can be a journey, daunting and all uphill
Good times come and go so fast but bad times
Hangin' around, stand still
It teases me as I get to the finishing line
Then trips me up, tumbling to the start
Tired, I begin again uphill, step by step
With a heavy heart.

Then I have my many blessings when I think of them
They remind me of my luck and lessen the load
Suddenly I don't feel so angry
As I begin down that old familiar road.

I think of all the things I have that money cannot buy
My daughter's love, my son's smile
That make me happy for more than just a little while
Then I remind myself that I am quite lucky
I may not have riches but I have my family, my health
To which a dying king
Will give up his all, kingdom and all, bargain all his wealth.

Yet still I will moan and yes I will groan
And yes, life will continue to seem unfair
But I promise that I will try to remember the many blessings
That come Hell or high water, will be unflagging and always be there.

Steve Prout

Miracles

Miracles sometimes happen - that's what people say
Look at the world we live in! A miracle in itself; Man's
Inventions; as we go about our lives, from the start of every day
'Til the end, miracles big and small surround; shifting sands,
Sea, sun, birds, beasts and flowers; from the day's first light
And dark night's end, we see the wonders of a miraculous world
There for all to enjoy; flocks of birds in formation flight
Fantastic creatures and plants under the ocean; exotic unfurled
Petals - magnificent trees; these wondrous creations,
Miracles no doubt. So miracles don't sometimes happen,
They are with us constantly; when our Lord walked this Earth,
He performed special miracles to prove God's love; and the greatest -
A mother's love, unconditional - so cherish - men, women, girls,
Boys - the most wonderful of all - the gift of motherly love a
Miracle more precious than life itself; as pure as a snow-white dove.

Valerie Hall

26th March

Floating

Spirit revolves silently
A soul floating within the eternal void
Awaiting the moment of the next rebirth
The attraction of the physical form, a chance to understand
But to leave the light will cause great anguish.
The longing is too powerful, the gravity of life winds
The octave of the heavenly voice begins the next cycle
'It is time'
The joining, to become one for love.
New forming child, spirit enters, heart is immersed in the divine
Heart joins the beat of its mother's, they speak as one
We share all it beats,
My mother's blood is mine,
My mother's food is mine,
My mother's voice is mine,
My mother's eyes are mine
My mother's thoughts are mine
The air that is breathed into my cells,
The love that is felt embracing me,
The tears that my mother sheds for her joy
We share all it beats
My mother's heart teaches me of her love
But also a whisper of another voice is contained within the heart,
We listen, it opens the whirling doorway,
It promises to leave it ajar, for my longing is great,
Understanding grows within, the voice from the void is recognised
You reside within your mother, your mother resides within me
You breathe through your mother, your mother breathes through me
Your heart resides in your mother, your mother's heart resides with me
You have become one with the voice of your mother's heart
I am that voice.

James Walsh

Angel

On a cliff edge, at a desolate space,
stood a beautiful woman,
with a gaunt, haunted face.
Tear-stained cheeks, and a heart filled with woe,
a mind that is pounding and telling her to go.
Go where there is peace,
and everything is bright.
No one is unhappy, cocooned in His light.
As the stars twinkle up in the sky
her mind thinks of memories,
and time that's gone by.
Laughter and love from a family so strong,
to leave them and hurt them
would all be so wrong.
Words will build bridges,
and mend broken hearts.
Bravery and courage,
will bring brand new starts:
She turns from the cliff top
no longer alone
an angel walks with her
on her way home ...

Annie Frame

27th March

Think Happy Thoughts

Whenever you are feeling low and nothing goes quite right,
don't let it drag you down some more, instead put up a fight.
And just to help you on your way, to get on top of things,
think happy thoughts and feel the lift I promise you it brings.

Think hot and sunny days and sandy beaches far away.
Think of the very favourite place where you would like to stay.
Think walking in the moonlight with the person whom you love
with nothing else to share your space except the stars above.

Think fondly of the good times shared together with a friend.
In fact just think of any way your time you'd rather spend.
Think only of those things that bring a calmness to your day.
Think happy thoughts for they will always help you on your way.

Tina Sanderson

28th March

Thank You

I want to tell you how I love you, but where to begin?
Sometimes hearing your laughter just makes me want to join in

Your eyes are deepest green, like from a tropical lagoon
That make my heart beat hard like something out of a cartoon

You are the most attractive woman I have ever seen
With beauty far beyond the limits of my wildest dreams

Whenever I am with you, every second spent I savour
My life lived if you leave would be like food without the flavour

A winter chill surrounds me whenever you are not around
My life spent without you would turn my whole world upside down

Us spending time together are still all my wishes granted
You only get one chance in life, so let's take full advantage

I love how you are, lady-like, it means a lot to me
Your greatest feature is your glowing personality

Even though we've been seeing each other now four years
You still make me so happy that I'm crying happy tears

Your heart is like a beacon that burns brighter than the sun
And your love for me shines out like rays of hope when I have none

You're so petite and delicate, which always makes me smile
I want to cover you in bubble wrap, labelled 'Fragile'

You are so kind and generous, you always keep on giving
I'm certain that without you, my life would not be worth living

There is no head unturned when we are out together walking
It makes me proud when they see that it's me to whom you're talking

You're so interesting, I linger on every word you say
When we're alone together, it's like Christmas every day

My love for you keeps growing with an incline ever steep
I wish each day would end so I can hold you when we sleep

Every gift that I could think of, I think this one is the finest
My love written in a poem, thanking you for all your kindness

TJR

28th March

Birdsong

Little bird, singing sweet
So high up in the tree -
Your harmonious tunes,
We can hear -
From the break of day until the sun sets.

You seem so fragile
Yet your powerful song can be heard
From miles around.
God made you so special -
And blessed you with such a powerful sound.

I sit in my garden,
Close my eyes -
Thanking God
For His creation.

Debbie Nobbs

29th March

The Beauty Of The Moon

Have you ever risen in the night when the moon is round and full;
When the garden is bathed in glorious light, and felt a compulsive pull
To step over the patio sill and walk on the silvered grass
While the rest of the world is quiet and still and the pond
Is a looking glass?

To stand by the beds of night-scented stock and breathe in
The fragrant air
And marvel at the lone dandelion clock that shines with a beauty, rare?
Have you stood in admiration of this wonderful ethereal scene
And listened with concentration for creatures oft heard but not seen?

There are those who worship the golden sun and fret
When it goes too soon
But in the small hours when day is done, I long for
The sight of the moon.
I resent the hours when I have to sleep that my body may be renewed
While the moon, unobserved, may her vigil keep
In her lonely celestial mood.

Eileen Martin

29th March

Follow Your Dreams

Give love in full measure
Give hope as a sign
Give faith to another
And give of your time

Take love as an honour
Take hope as the truth
Take faith as protection
And friendship as proof

Keep love in your life
Keep hope in your schemes
Keep faith with your future
And follow your dreams.

Alison J Mannion

A Special Cake

Just take some sense of humour
Stir in some love as well
Then add a touch of tolerance
That's vital I hear tell

And don't forget some tender care
And leaven it with respect
A hand that's there to help always
Will have profound effect.

There is no room for prejudice
Just caring deep support
An ounce of understanding
Quite quickly should be brought

Attach some liberalism
And fairness don't forget
Then patience in great quantity
To help the mixture set

Some noble generosity
Of stamina, a lot
Together with indulgence
And toughness just a shot

Large helping of emotion
Deep passion in there too
Top off with great devotion
Now it's all there for you

So what has been accomplished?
Where were ingredients heading?
They make a special wholesome cake
To mark your Golden Wedding.

Enid Gill

31st March

Silently I Go

I love to walk in the snow, silently I go
I love to watch the sunset and see the red glow
I love to hear a robin sing and see his red breast
And watch the blackbird fly to its nest
I love to watch the blue tit flit from tree to tree
Singing a little song so silently
I love to walk in the woods, silently I go
Walking on the leaf mould rotting down below
I love to see the holly leaves shining in the sun
I think oh what a lovely world since time begun
It is so sad to think all this is being spoilt by greed
And awful wars man does make causing so much heartache
I think to myself when silently I go if man did really know
What he is doing to our wonderful world
Why can't he be like a beautiful tree
Reaching out his arms for all to see and love
And all share peace like the skylark up above
If only what a wonderful world it could be.

Kath Gay

Evensong

In the west the sunset's cauldron
Smoulders on the day's flaked ashes,
Across the blank page of evening sky
A taut sentence of birds dashes,
And the epitaph of the day flows
In feathered wings to the western keep.
Knowing the loved day hymned to rest
My heart, too, folds its wings in sleep.

Pamela Constantine

Perhaps

'Maybe' we say, or just 'perhaps',
Some words of intervention.
Then realise, with second thoughts,
There is no clear intention!
For 'yes' or 'no' it's simple,
No arguments at all.
It's crystal clear to anyone,
The writing's on the wall!
So go back to the question,
Was it really quite so hard?
'Perhaps' to say you're sorry,
Or 'maybe' send a card!
'Yes' might be too dramatic,
'No' too definite by half.
'Maybe' was much more suitable,
'Perhaps' you'd make them laugh!
Remind me of the question,
'Maybe' I'll understand.
'Perhaps' it was too difficult
To say, 'You're looking grand!'

T G Bloodworth

To Find Love

Love is in the forest, the mountains and the sea.
Love is in the tiny ant, the donkey and the bee.
Love is in the raindrop, the sunshine and the snows,
Love is in the heart of man, no matter where he roams.

To *find* the love in forests, take a walk alone.
Inhale the scent of pine trees. See squirrel - glimpse a fawn.
Touch the myriad blossoms - hear the songbirds call.
Listen to the insects - watch leaves, like feathers fall.

To *find* the love in mountains, climb the highest peak.
Glorify their beauty, which to you will speak.
Feel the strength beneath you, a million years to form,
And in these few quiet moments, communion will be born.

To *find* the love in oceans, go out there in a boat.
Sense the depths below you - fathoms on which you float.
Hear the call of dolphin, see mighty whales swim by,
Feel the joy beneath you, where many creatures lie.

To *find* the love in skies on high, just stand and look above.
For God has painted there for us, a picture filled with love.
A vast and wondrous canvas, upon which can be seen,
The stars, the sun and planets ... our silver moon, serene.

To *find* the love in hearts of men, just take a look inside ...
For your heart's a reflection of what no man can hide.
Though some may say they know not love, this is their own lie
For inside each and all of us, the spark of love can't die.

So *look for love* inside yourself - send it round about.
Give of love to those of us who feel they are without.
Don't hide your love, or hoard it. That's not what it's for.
Open up and share it - that way *you'll get more* ...

Patricia B Spear

Smile

He smiled at me this morning,
My autistic son.
At me, his mum.
Not at my right temple,
Right shoulder, left earlobe.
Not at the lampshade,
The bedhead, the wardrobe.
But eyeball to eyeball -
What a shock, what a joy.
My first full on smile
From my twelve-year-old boy.
He soon looked away.
It didn't last long
But my heart surged inside me
And I burst into song.
No more than a glimmer.
Doesn't seem very much
But for me, it's like Midas:
A bright golden touch.
From no hope to progress,
From write-off to maybe.
The start of a future.
The end of my baby.

Dee Gordon

Refracted Light

R ainbow colours fill the sky
A rcing hues way up high
I ndigo, red, orange and green
N ew beauty have I seen
B eneath clouds dull grey
O pulent colours on display
W hence forth after April showers

Peter G H Payne

3rd April

Finding Faith

To pick a faith is not as easy as anyone might think,
And then it up and fails you and your heart begins to sink,
I used to think the faith I chose would give me what I need,
But in the end, finding faith and keeping it did the trick.

Margaret McGinty

Come To Me

(Come to me, all you who are weary. Matthew 11:28)

Come to Me all you that labour
And I will give you rest.
The burden that I place on you
Will always be the best.
And if you choose to learn of Me
To follow in My way
You'll find the strength to do the things
That you have heard Me say.
You'll love your God with all your heart
Your neighbour as you should
And praise His name with every breath,
You think, *If I just could.*
You can, if to the Lord Himself
Your sins you gladly give
And, by His grace, He'll show you
How you can start to live.

Patricia Patterson

Sinking Back Up

A heavy heart
Pulls me down
Like a ton of iron
Sinking into the ocean,
Down it goes
Stinging my skin
With a confused
Brain organ,
Hush, I tell my mind
Just for a moment or two
To let my body rest
From this uproaring commotion.

In the depths of nowhere
In a place no one cares
My limbs are chained
And nothingness is weighed
Down here I was pulled
'Destiny,' I was told
But I know one thing will undo
Verb 'to say' to verb 'to do';
Pray to the Almighty God
And a ray of light will shine abroad
Never fear to pray
For praying kills fear and hope revives, I dare say
Chains will unleash
Like wood you'll float back to the beach
Air you will breathe
As God, your calls have reached.

Janan Robin Zaitoun

Squirrels

They nibble away and chatter,
Leaping from branch to branch of the trees,
In the woods they scatter,
As they dabble away from the bees.

In bluebell woods with bark so high,
They stop and listen to those that spy,
Running away with furtive foot,
They crawl up the bark as we stand and look.

With spring in the air, they nibble with pride
At the last nuts left from the open skies,
Then as they turn towards the night,
I watch and wonder at this great sight.

Rosemary E Pearson

6th April

The Offering

When you hear those sirens, offer up a prayer
For the guidance of those injured
And those who are trying to care.
A prayer for courage to deal with the sadness,
Or the joy - it could be a maternity dash -
Congrats! You've got a boy!
But a family might have lost
The most important person in their lives.
Offer up a prayer that God will hear their cries.
Amen.

J W Whiteacre

7th April

Green Fields In The Rain

Green fields and rain, the perfect blend,
Kaleidoscope of beauty, unsurpassed
By the wonders of sunlight.
Water dripping from freshly-bathed branches;
Leaves sparkling in green splendour.

Bark of trees in varying shades of russet;
Lush, rain-laden grass
Glistening like a vast emerald carpet,
Recently laundered.
The freshness of everything
Stimulates the senses.

Magnificent array of field flowers,
Washed for the occasion;
Cowslips, buttercups, daisies and thistles
Blossom under the supernatural aura
Of the rainbow whose dipping arc fades
Into the distant, radiant undergrowth.

Dark pools at the edge of the wood,
Peppered with ebullient raindrops;
The colourful chaffinch and green linnet
Soaking themselves in a flurry
Of feathered propulsion.

As the dark clouds fade on the horizon,
The warmth returns
And all is calm again.
The pungent smell of the countryside
Makes one feel happy to be alive.

Hugh J Lynch

Rome - April 2005

Papa John Paul
embraced all humanity
- unconditionally.
Deep understanding
and the rare ability
to warm the hearts of everyone
- a true man of God
in our riddled world.
Never flinching from his duties
we all witnessed
his immense suffering.
We were humbled and moved
by his honesty
and devotion.
His eyes seeing all,
inviting participation and love.
His successor cannot hide
from the global village,
the doors are now
irrevocably open wide.
Papa John Paul's presence
and open arms remain with us.

Margaret Ann Wheatley

Spring

(Written for my mother-in-law, April 2001)

How I love this time of year!
Daffodils trumpeting golden cheer,
Tulips parted to kiss the air,
Sweetly scented by hyacinths there.
Blossom's soft blanket of pink and white,
Evenings milder, long and light,
Buds and bulbs bursting with glee,
Birds sing their songs with new energy.
Little green shoots reach for the sun,
Stretching their arms, life's race has begun,
Daisies and buttercups grab their chance,
And litter my lawn with their crazy dance.
Regal magnolia, so handsome and proud,
Bowing and waving to please the crowd,
And colours, colours, splash the scene,
Rainbows erupting from out of the green.
Such magic and wonder reminds me you're near,
How I love this time of year!

Michele Amos

The Returning Rain

The rain arrives in a downpour,
To quench the hot, dry earth.
The ground, baked stone-hard,
Over many sun-drenched weeks,
Initially rejects much of the deluge.
The run-off forms shallow pools,
And fast-running streamlets,
Converting dust to liquid mud.
Red soil running as rivers of blood,
That my distant ancestors called,
'Mother Gaea's annual blood feast'.
The purveyor of all things good,
Which brings back life,
To the welcoming earth.
Sludge slowly seeping down,
Into fractures, cracks and crevices.
Simple soakaways; the ground heals.
Water drains into the depths below,
Stirring sleeping seeds to germinate,
Whilst worms squirm in pure pleasure.
Dormant microbes and fungi,
Stimulated, begin to multiply.
From the bleeding dirt,
Arises a sweet aroma,
So blessed and refreshing,
That the locals throw open,
Newly washed windows and doors.
The dust at last suppressed.
The sun finally breaks through.
Roused nature touches the divine.

John Pegg

Hymn To A Friend

Blessings galore,
light may your spirits be;
friendship transcends
storm, tempest
and the wildest sea.

Despite the darkest shadows,
clouds and rain,
you helped me sparkle,
laugh and soar again.

Malcolm Williams

11th April

Drop Of Dew

Dew for you, my precious one
Springing forth beneath that sun,
Causing grass blades to topple o'er
Mini fountains then mini floods.
Sparkle of hope, yes, joy and peace
Provided from Heaven
It will never cease
Our minds to amaze -
What wonderful dampness
Now glorious dawn
With each of her workers
Hanging on to drops of dew
From the Lord, to you.

Jac Simmons

11th April

The Lord Speaks To Me

The Lord speaks to me as I take up my pen,
and tells me the words I should write,
He fills me with ideas for poems and rhymes
through the day and for most of the night.
He shows me the wonderful things to behold,
and helps me to choose the right words.
His hands guide my scribbles in all that I do,
in sentence and chapter and verse.
His voice is the rainbow after the storm,
each colour, each wonder, each fear,
it is the child's laughter, the call of the bird,
each sunrise, each nightfall, each tear.
The Lord speaks to me as I take up my pen,
all through the day and the night.
I know I was blessed on the day of my birth
to sit myself quietly - and write.

J P Henderson-Long

12th April

Loved Ones Lost

How do you go through life,
When family and friends are no longer there?
How do you get out of bed,
With just four walls at which to stare?
How do you greet the morning,
Of each and every day?
How do you feel as night draws in,
With no goodnights to say?
How do you hold back the tears,
Weighing heavy on your heart?
How do you feel? Lost and alone,
Well it's time to make a new start.

Loved ones lost would never want
Your heart not ever to mend,
Life's too short, it's time to move on
A new life's just around the bend,
There are plenty of people left in this world
Lost souls like you and me,
It's time to go out and make new friends
With time, it gets better, you'll see,
The key to unlock the grief that we feel
And help us over time,
Is to never forget our loved ones lost
And that moving on is no crime.

Ashley O'Keefe

Chart Him Number One

Once in a while, or maybe all day
you think of our Saviour
who once came our way
you would sing the great hymns
of Jesus and then
all is forgotten until when?

You have a problem with no one to share it
yet this is not strictly true
for our Saviour above
will kindle your love
this may seem a miracle
to you.

Through prayer you can reach Him
for He is there in the wings
and His love is ongoing always
with Him as your guide and trusted friend
chart Him now, as your number one.

Hazel Sheppard

12th April

The Wonders Of This World

Don't be fooled by what others
Say or perceive to be
The wonders of this world

For they exist and can be found
In the most unlikely places
Tear up the travel brochures
There's no need to join
The caravan of tourists
Thirsty for instant culture

You can find your own
Maybe find another who shares
The same belief and joy
Anytime, anywhere,
No, better make that
Sometime, somewhere
Look out your window
Look into yourself
But never lose the will to look

The wonders of this world
A vision so complete
As to suffocate and demand
Total allegiance from
Those who come to gaze
Drawn to such a flame

Such beauty, such fragility
So much as to be immense
The wonders of this world

Richard Gould

Thank You

(Dedicated to Roger Fudge)

Drawn by precious sapphire eyes inscribed
With Heaven's grace, guide me safely.
My fingertips trace your nose, each touch
Illustrating perfection that soon reveals
Your saccharine lips, tongue-shaping L,
Curving O into V, and rolling E as your voice whispers, 'Love ... '

Your slender chin leads my gaze to your neck,
Smooth as romance draping rose petals,
And the shape modelled on your arms
Awakens new emotions, illuminating my heart.
Steady wrists joined to masculine hands
That propose nights of tranquillity and arouse my curiosity;
Luring thoughts, secrets, from my soul to take wing from my lips.

My spirit flickers in awe of God's artistry
Elegantly standing before me and I find my hands
Gently reaching through the essence of serenity coiling around you
And they caress your beautifully sculpted body
As I drift into your protective embrace.

I feel your soothing touch upon my back
And your fingers glide through each strand of my hair
While you sing bittersweet gothic melodies
And your heart echoes the tantalising rapture, which seduced me
And the creeping shadows retreat to their gnarled covens of Hell
As you have swept my life back into the light.

Jessica E Stapleton

13th April

Spread The News

The time has come, the news to spread
That Christ has risen from the dead
And through His pain and misery
Believers are from sin set free

Redemption's price is fully paid
There is no need to feel afraid
Just ask our Saviour to come in
He will cleanse you of all sin

So as through this life you go
Let the folks you meet all know
Help the doubters understand
That life with Jesus Christ is grand

Tell them of the joy you found
Of the pleasures that abound
As you walk with Christ each day
For He is with you all the way

Until on Earth your life does end
He will always be your friend
And then as you cease to roam
Your Lord will safely guide you home

Ian Russell

The Worth Of Thorns

Strut as you will, or criticise,
It's a waste of time,
The time that flies.
Love will triumph.
As He was born,
To show us all,
The worth of Thorns,
Circling round His tender head,
He left the rose of love instead,
So grasp the thorns, to know the rose,
All are to Heaven
Predisposed.

Mary Hughes

14th April

Lilford Park, September 2005

Nature nurtures me
Silence surrounds me
Saying no to all negativity
Sitting under these trees.

Sitting in solitude
Beneath dreaming trees
Peace lies beside me
Holding my hand
Calming me down.

All around I hear sweet harmonies
Nature's music takes me higher
I stare into an Indian summer sky
Upside down, deep blue sea, sky.

Closing my eyes to visualise
Meditating, repeating my mantra
Om, mani, padmi, hum
Om, mani, padmi, hum.

Nature nurtures me
Silence surrounds me
In Lilford Park, September 2005
A beautiful dream comes true.

Ian Bosker

The Swing

Can you see the swing beneath the tree?
Can you see the sparrows fluttering free,
And the white clouds scudding through the sky,
Or the grassy bank where the crocus lie?

Can you hear the sound of the taxi's horn,
Or the cry of a baby newly born?
See the swaying curls in a young girl's hair?
Can you smell her perfume in the air?

Take a barefoot walk on the morning grass.
Can you hear the bell for morning Mass
And see folk wending their way
To the local church on Easter day?

Will you count these blessings manifold,
Or wait until you're much too old
To give your thanks, or plan ahead?
Will you see the light when you are dead?

Did you ever wonder when in prayer
That maybe He might not be there?
Open your eyes if you want to see.
Can you see the swing beneath the tree?

Bernard Brady

15th April

Transitions

The seamless robe Your mother made
Fashioned by skilful, loving hands
The product of a caring heart -
(No seams Your tender flesh could stand)
So dazzling bright on Tabor's mound
Lies soiled and bloodstained on the ground

Ascending to Your Father's arms
With trumpet blast and joyful shout
As You approach Your kingly throne
The brightness of Your robe shines out

On Christening day my soul was bright
Bathed - like Your robe - in lustrous light
Ere careless life and sinful ways
Had dimmed or even quenched its rays
Yet when the hourglass of my life
Has emptied its last grains of sand
You who gave up Your life for me
Will mercy give with Your pierced hand
So will my brightness be restored
In peace by our ever loving Lord.

Mary Rafferty

16th April

The Risen Christ

Chris is risen, alleluia,
What a privilege for me,
As I see that empty cross,
From my sins can forgiven be.

God gave us *His* son,
That a new life we could start,
And by seeking out *His* plan,
We can do our part.

Through prayer we can know that plan,
So seek it every day,
Then with Christ's help, do it,
It could help others on their way.

Christ's love is not just for us,
He wants us to spread it round,
And by our very actions,
That love could soon be found.

So make today that starting point,
Christ will help you through,
And it will be a big surprise,
What your acts will do.

Whether they be small or large,
This one thing is for sure,
Once you get started,
You will want to do much more.

Will A Tilyard

16th April

Easter Sunday

Look at Christ upon the cross
See the suffering, see the pain
But do not despair.
Christ crucified
Christ died
Christ rose again; alleluia, allelulia.
Christ lives in you
Christ lives in me
So let us all good Christians be
And take to all who know Him not
The peace, the love, the joy that comes
Through the glorious resurrection of
Jesus Christ our Lord. Alleluia.
We too, by our baptism in Christ have
Died and arisen. Praise Him, alleluia.
So let us go forward to share
The wonderful gifts He has given.
Easter is a time of hope and promise
Let us rejoice in the beautiful, glorious resurrection
Of Jesus Christ our Lord. Alleluia, alleluia, alleluia.

M Cubis

Today

(Numbers 6:24-26 NIV)

May the Son of God enfold you
In His merciful embrace;
May the Son of God enfold you
And shine His light upon your face.

May the Son of God enfold you
And strengthen you in all ways;
May the Son of God enfold you
And bless you all your days.

May the Son of God enfold you
Ever wrap you in His light;
May the Son of God enfold you
For you are precious in His sight!

Firecloud

17th April

A New Day

A new day is dawning, greet the morning
Just say a prayer, in God's care
You have been through the darkest hours of night
Now it is morning light

Now a new day starts for you to live
To it your best you must always give
Not very inviting is the straight road
But it will lead to a safe abode

Little lanes which go off beat
With much pleasure you may greet
Just beware - there may be a snare
For guidance - say a prayer

As you travel along
Sing a song
Give a smile as you proceed on your road of life
Beware of trouble and strife
And say a prayer for God's love and care.

D Huff

Joy

Jesus is joy and peace,
Jesus is wisdom and grace,
God loves you!

I worship You Father forever,
In Jesus' holy name!
Holy Spirit, take over,
Spirit of Jesus, guide me;
Come, bring Your fire,
Into my heart, so cold!

When Jesus died,
The temple veil was torn in tow -
We can all come to God,
By Jesus Christ!

God has provided
Atonement for our sins -
Our High Priest Jesus!
Praise God!

Ilan Micah Block

19th April

Finding Peace

Come to me now, Lord, Your heart keeps me warm:
I need You with me to weather this storm.
I'm just a sinner, but dear Lord I pray,
'Please give me strength, just to live one more day.'

Show me compassion, my heartache dispel.
Dear Lord, please take me from my living hell.
God with Your power, please show me Your might
In my dark tunnel, let me see Your light.

Come to me now, Lord, my dark disappears;
Take me where love is, a land with no fears.
Open my eyes, so I'm no longer blind;
Show me Your heart, so Your peace I can find.

Pardon my doubting, keep me in Your sight;
Come to me now, Lord, guide me through this night.

Des Beirne

Eternal Glory

Let's turn to Him whose love embraces
The countless throngs of many races,
Who gave us life and mind and power,
Who shaped the eagle and the flower.

He is majestic, wise, far-seeing
The core and source of every being,
He made a myriad suns and stars,
Yet men persist in waging wars.

He is the Lord of peace sublime
Beyond the reach of space and time,
A master artist who delights
In he who's gentle, not who fights.

You can in troubled times oft pray
To Him who comforts, shows the way,
Be grateful for His gifts galore,
Source of all riches held in store.

He cares for every sparrow's fall,
Have you just heard His loving call
To come to Him, to love and serve
Along the path, not twist or swerve?

Let us fill up our days with grace
That we may see our Maker's face,
And through life's trials to discern
The spring of joy for which hearts yearn.

We are not orphans and our dad
Will see us through this world gone mad,
Come to the light through work or play,
He'll change our darkness into day.

Emmanuel Petrakis

Look Again

Look up and view the sky
Just see how blue
Look up and view the stars
Just see how clear

Look across and view the sea
Just see how smooth
Look across and view the field
Just see the space

Look around and view the face
Just see the glow
Look around and view my eyes
They see the best

Clare Price

Reaching Out

Imagine life without a friend.
Difficult perhaps to comprehend.
No one to talk to, no one to care,
Intimate thoughts and feelings to share.

No one to turn to in time of need,
No one at hand on your behalf to plead.
No consolations in time of sorrow,
No expectations of a better tomorrow.

Reaching out, seeking affection,
But no response, only rejection.
Living in an uncaring society,
Tainted with selfishness and impropriety.

We are not, by nature, all gregarious,
Some are reticent, some self-conscious.
Whatever our disposition ... in the end,
We all need someone as a friend.

Shouldn't we therefore be more caring?
Seek out those who need a little loving,
Offer the hand of friendship and be proud,
To befriend those lonely ... even in a crowd.

So, let's try and be a ray of brightness,
To be a shining light in someone's darkness,
It's just a kindly word or deed,
That's often all you ever need.

Bryn Phillips

Untitled

I look with awe and reverence at the night sky,
The comet silently passing by,
The connectedness of the universe, filling me with love,
I reach out from within and pull the stars to myself,
Immersing in the joy of belonging,
Anxieties and fears evaporate,
As the life pulse beckons,
An eternal spiral of dust and decay,
Forever changing, renewing.

Janet Rocher

God's Love

When you are down and you are blue
Remember God still loves you
He is always there to hold your hand
To try and make you understand
That all we have in life is love
Sent to us from Heaven above
So why don't you put on a smile?
Love is around you all the while.

Robin Morgan

Marathon

London in spring blooms
Slowly but hugely,
Opening its sights, sounds, perfumes
Till they drown the puny senses.
London in spring is matchless
In the garden of world capitals,
A mighty rose
Big, but perfect in its parts
Like Juno harmonising bulk and beauty.
Look into its centre,
Breathe deep, observe,
Hear the heavy pounding
On an April day -
A mighty orchestra of feet
Beat out their throbbing symphony
From east to west
Close packed in the park
Lassoing Cutty Sark,
Making thunder on Tower Bridge
East Enders all,
Then westward
Failing, but driven on,
A selfless army,
Pain-wracked host of givers.
Pheidippedes was first;
He gave his life
To bring good news to Athens;
Thousands since have given ease of body
To bring ease of mind to all.

Philip Worth

Day By Day

Day by day we lead our life
In this world of war and strife
Everything is done with speed
Often touched by lust and greed

If only we all paused - and thought
Why are we so tense and fraught?
Why not lend a hand to others?
After all, we are all brothers

It doesn't have to be too much
A friendly smile, a gentle touch
If instead of take, take, take
We learn to give - for God's own sake

To give and not to count the cost
Then all would never be quite lost
This world would be a better place
If we helped each other through life's race

Mavis Johnson

Dawn Chorus

Listen to the birdsong in forests' lofty heights,
Singing out their melodies of joy and sheer delight.
Praise that echoes through the branches, touching every tree,
Glad to be alive they trill in gladsome harmony.
Each one tells a story of God's grand and perfect plan,
Showing how he warrants the heartfelt praise of man.
If birds can offer thankfulness in such a simple way,
Surely man should do the same beneath God's holy sway.

There is so much to praise for as we look around and see,
All the grand provision God provides for you and me.
Each day has its measure of unlimited supply,
E'en in midst of trouble He is there. Who can deny?
Waiting to uphold us if we give Him chance to show,
His love for His creation, as the birds must surely know!
They accept and worship as an everyday routine,
Let us join in praising Him, our part in this great scheme!

Maybe our affluent way of life forgets that man is lost,
Without the God who made us and saved us at great cost!
That praise should be the centre of each and every day,
In thankfulness for blessing showered upon our earthly way
And blessings come in many guises - sometimes we do not know,
That deep within life's problems is the means to help us grow,
In understanding of the power that rules all man's concerns
And brings him ever closer to the truth for which he yearns.

Arise at dawn and listen to the chorus nature sings,
Lift the heart in worship and know the joy this brings.
Nothing else can satisfy the searching, longing heart,
Than joining with creation to do our feeble part.
It's worth the early effort to lift the mind above
And concentrate all thoughts upon God's never-ending love,
To start the day in praise to Him whate'er our circumstance,
Therein lies the answer for each hour to be enhanced!

Elizabeth Bruce

Time

(Dedicated to my friend, Carole)

Life is strange, don't you think?
As the hours continue,
Every day we start anew
And years fly by in a blink.

Sometimes I think time goes so slow,
Sometimes I think time goes so fast,
Sometimes I sit and think of the past,
Then sometimes I just keep on the go.

It's strange how one feels to wait for a date,
And wondering just how good it will be,
With great new places and new people to see.
Then, when dates come so fast, you wish time could wait.

Just like the dentist's appointment, one always dreads,
And afterwards the great feeling of being free.
Like the hospital appointment; oh no, please not me,
And then wishing one could have stayed safe in bed instead.

It's funny, when you're enjoying gardening, or some chore,
Time seems to go so much quicker than you thought it would do;
And yet, those nasty, repetitive chores, and washing-up too,
Seem to make the time slow down to an intolerable bore.

We would all like to have plenty of time, till the end of the line,
And even one small minute has gone forever, throughout the day;
Never to be relived again, as we journey along life's way.
So we have to try and enjoy every minute of our precious time.

Doreen Ranson

25th April

Day's End

The hoot of an owl signals the end of the day,
As in night's sky appears the awesome Milky Way.
Sparkling stars peering down at humanity's lair,
As you look up and wonder, is anyone up there?
The howl of a lonely dog baying at the moon,
The silence of highways so eerie in the gloom.
Long stretches of solitude, vehicles out of use,
Resting until called upon to again let loose.
Peace in the nursery full of inert games and toys,
As the innocents lie dreamless, young girls and boys.
A hollow footstep passing, as a latecoming seeks rest,
The silence heavy as birds curl, warm in the nest.
Last thoughts of the day as you retire with a yawn,
Lock up and switch off as you salute the oncoming dawn.
Let out the cat as he parades and impatiently waits,
To pursue the latest conquest on his private estate.
Another day at an end, the world's problems still there,
As you relax in your sweet corner, hoping to share
Another dawn, tomorrow amid life's hectic stream,
Before you slip ever deeper into your land of dreams.

George Carrick

Finding Faith

O thou of little faith
Put your trust in me
And when the darkest shadows fall
Your light I will be
And when everything is going wrong
And you have lost the way
Seek me your god whate'er your creed
And lift your eyes and pray
And I will lead along the path
Out of your confusion
Until you find the answers
And make the resolution
That faith is your solution.

Roland Seager

27th April

Magic Moments

Look for the magic in your life,
Don't be overcome by toil and strife,
Magic moments when they happen to you,
Often come right out of the blue
And they are sometimes quite effective
At putting things in perspective.

A Cooper

27th April

Mother Nature

(Dedicated to my family who 'mothered' me and gave me good values. Love Kitty)

At break of dawn I wander round and look
And feel the calm of vibrant running brook
As it meanders round each cosy nook.
Catch the warmth of sun upon my face
Displaying His might and grace
And as I pause and pray in this meaningful space.
'Take the universe in your hand
Crush it like grains of sand
Rebuild it, make it new
Show mankind what you can do!
Command obedience to you.
Take the evil from mankind today
Prepare them to follow your guided way.

Trace our lives upon the sand
Take our destinies firmly in hand.
Teach us love of fellow men
Go deeply into every tarnished mind
Help us develop a kinship that is loving and kind.'

A Yap-Morris

28th April

Nature's Garden

I like a sense of casual profusion
With not too much of man's intrusion.
The rage to grow
Must be controlled, just so
And yet, the urge to bud and bloom and seed
Must be allowed, so great is nature's need to breed.
But beware of chaos and confusion
It only leads to weed pollution.
So plan your borders
To meet with nature's orders,
And be grateful for her lavish hand
In creating all that you have planned.
Be not too neat
For that way lies sad grey defeat.
When aphids swarm
And snails perform
Their lacy patterns on your hosta
Just remember that it's nature's roster
To feed her children in your garden.
So, if you must, be gently ruthless and ask her pardon
As you prune and snip and tweak and trim,
Your chance of winning is quite slim!

Eileen M Lodge

The Rhythm Of Life

Today I saw a wondrous sight -
A skein of geese in graceful flight
Calling as they rose
On powerful wings
Into the distant hills -
Just one of nature's 'little things'.

Then swallows circling in the sky
Skimming, darting, twittering as they fly
Getting ready to migrate
Excitedly they congregate
Small black shapes against the sky
As autumn comes they say, 'Goodbye.'

Mist-laden winds and autumn hues
Of gold and brown and red
Tell us that winter soon will come
When everything seems dead.

But nature's only sleeping
To wake again in spring
With marvellous renewal
Of trees, flowers, everything.

Diana Price

30th April

Life's Tapestry

Glitter and gold and glamour and such
Life's treasures to hold on to that mean so much
But the mind's data bank is the most precious of all
That regurgitates the priceless when put on recall
So harvest your moments in life's tapestry store
So your winters are warm with a rich memory store.

Doris Hoole

1st May

Look To The Hills

Look to the hills every morning
Mist softly clings like a glove
Gradually rising, dispersing
As sun beams stream from above.

Look to the hills at high noon time
Clouds gather, chasing the sun,
Changing the blue sky of Heaven
To overcast grey clouds as one.

Look to the hills every evening
Long shadows merging to bring
God's glory of sun setting splendour
Birds now fly west on the wing.

Look to the hills when you're troubled
Forever steadfast they stand,
Strong, solid and reassuring
Like watch towers over the land.

Look to the hills as the night winds
Blow breezes across darkened skies
Yet moonbeams and starlight shine brightly
Powered by God's watchful eye.

Look to the hills as the seasons
Change, see the patterns unfold
Green in the springtime and summer
Russet, before autumn gold.

Then on the hills in the winter
White, frosty trees standing tall,
Silently waiting for rebirth
God's rainbow of promise spans all.

Joan Heybourn

Untitled

First whiff of May
Hints of greening borne on a breeze
Golden dandelion wheels
Clandestine rabbit litters midst gardeners' prize patches
Blackthorn pinpoint blossoms

Six-thirty now
A stag basking on red-green tufts rises
hugging the foxes' bracken realm
for a moment halts
wary, ears quivering
yet again bounds through dawn dazzle
beryl-bright as the sun strikes
lights up
glorifies him
follows his elusiveness
past a tracery of firs

Out of nowhere
Aiming nowhere
Like a gun salute for some royal birth
a cuckoo call explodes overhead
pert, joyous, utterly sure
Two bell-like notes
swing
through the space of a psalm
jolt us into
praise

Françoise de Pierpont

Your Beauty

My Lord,
I have received so much
When I could give nothing.
I am still given more than I can receive.
Even my desire to respond to You is Your gift.
Your royal prodigality confuses
This little volcanic woman, dabbler in dreams.
The sea is a pond of translucent luminosity.
My Lord,
Without You, beauty, wisdom, love
Leave my mouth dry.
But with You the garden here
Dressed by this morning of May,
The birds sounding in the branches,
The many rays of light drying the colourful washing
Reaching everyone and everywhere,
Irradiating from the dazzling sun,
Give me an inkling of the marvellous love
That prompted You to begin the grand project of creation.
Undeterred by sin, in the garden of Gethsemane;
Wrenched by agony and abandonment,
With Your sweated blood washed clean
Your creation to restore and fulfil its primal beauty.
My Saviour, praise and glory for this terrestrial paradise regained.

Angela Cutrale Matheson

On a Mayday morn
I arose at dawn
And walked over the meadow
To the sea.

The sun had come
On the house from the east,
The chaffinch and blackbird
Had sung beneath my window.

The lambs and ewes
In the pasture,
Stood back to back
For comfort.

The plough and horses
With gulls wheeling
Made a wondrous sight.

Lapwings on passage bent
Came in a cloud of fluttering wings,
The curlews whistled a greeting
As I reached the shore.

Oyster catchers, black and white
Like parsons,
Poked in the seaweed
For breakfast.

The air had a zest to it
Salt-tasting, under the sun,
All this wonder?
The day had just begun.

Time is all we need
In order to see
God ... in all His majesty.

Avis Nixon

The Cuckoo's Song

I woke up to the cuckoo's song
one tulip, April morning
and list' enraptured
lest his song
should vanish without warning.

On hearing his perennial tune
I *knew* that daffodils would bloom
and all the merry sounds of May
would promise soon
a summer's day -

(And what sheer beauty
in this certainty
that fills glad hearts
in you and me!)

We *know* each year the grass will grow;
that we can reap, just as we sow -
that summertime will follow spring
and bring fresh joy to everything ...
and summer seas will bid us 'Come!'
to dapple toes in morning sun -
and fields of ripening harvests bear
the joyous truth that God *is* there ...

Hannah Yates

6th May

Dream Catching

Swirling mists, snowy fog, faces stare at me,
Telling fortunes of the day, blind, these things I cannot see.
Voices shout, some whisper too, telling tales fair,
Visions of streets and cobbled ways, crinoline dresses flair.
A greying smile, thin lank hair, you mouth words I understand,
Flashing globes fill my head, reaching out I touch your hand.
Blinking eyes, I clear my mind, trying not to shake my head,
Grasping hard, I hear hidden thoughts: Conversations with the dead.
Marching orders; dull thud fire, echoes of the night,
Stinging, running, bloodshot eyes, I wish that I could fight.
Twilight beeches; scattered men; the slain and injured cry,
A flash of light, my knuckles white, pain makes me want to die.
Twitching; writhing, the sheets I pull, wrestling with my dreams,
Clandestine shapes mock my fate; silver tunnels make me scream.
Grasping tight, my comfort neigh, dripping sweat, I clutch and claw,
For some sweet memory, tranquil days, as pastel pictures draw.
Stone steps appear, leading up, glistening in the rain,
I hear a shout, thundering hooves, see urchins by a drain.
Silhouettes dance around a tree, Maypole garlands bright,
Full moon candles flicker strong; chanting their god's might.
Startled, waking, listening out; the visions fade away,
I'll try again to catch my dream; next time it may just stay.

Josh Brittain

Spring

You have arrived; I can hear your song,
I have missed you; you've been away too long.
I dreamt about you behind my closed door
And I wondered if we would meet once more.

Your beauty glitters under a sea of gold,
What a wondrous sight you are to behold.
Your warm breath gently caresses my face,
Making my senses pulsate at a very fast pace.

Birds' arias resound through the air
And people stop to listen and to stare.
Your colourful skirts sway in elegant flight,
Making our hearts fill with thankful delight.

The sun lays its golden carpet all around;
Flowers in colourful profusion abound
Winter has loosened its icy grip upon our Earth
And in its place spring brings a feeling of mirth.

Christine Potts

The Cherry Trees

And suddenly I saw them
The trees so full of light,
Wild and white the cherry blossom
In the May-time sun.

I see pictures in the branches
Where the sky peeps through,
A pretty Eastern maiden
With blossom in her hair
And figures there so blue, so white,
From a Chinese willow plate
And angels too, with pearly wings
Riding on the crystal air.

There can be no greater beauty,
Anywhere for me
Than the purest, whitest blossom
Of the cherry tree.

Ellen M Lock

Tread Softly

Tread softly on the moss of time
that hides those gentle footsteps, mine,
and know my child
I too have passed this way
in long forgotten, far-off days.

In search of light,
my journey's told,
my heart like yours,
young and bold,
but all that's left are words as these,
and whispers in the wizened trees,
that speak for me to souls not blind,
and those who seek hope's tranquil signs.
So,
grow in peace, heart's child of mine,
and glean wisdom from
those memories,
those footsteps that hide
beneath the moss of time.

Jean Caldwell

10th May

My Musical Thoughts

If I want to see a winter scene, the trees all around,
The cold north wind, the snow on the ground,
Sibelius for me.

If I want to see the month of May,
Beethoven's Pastoral for me today.

If I want to see the moon on the sea,
Debussy's La Mer today for me.

If I want to be quiet and thoughtful,
Then a Brahms Symphony is the thing for me.

If I want to be happy and gay,
Mozart or Haydn for me today.

But when I'm in the depths of despair
It's 'The Messiah' I listen to,
He's always there.

Joan Green

To Know You Is To Love You

(This poem is written for and dedicated to a very special little girl from Derry, Ireland. Her name is Caitlin Deane)

Your hair is long and beautiful
Your eyes are large and full of love
How lucky this world is to have in it
This special gift from up above
There's not a being in your life
Who hasn't been touched by you
For your soul is pure and precious
And your heart is kind and true
Your smile would light up the darkest skies
And your laughter is like music so sweet
You're a bundle of unconditional love
From your head right down to your feet
It's a privilege to know and to love you
But the biggest privilege by far
Is to know that you love us right back, Caitlin
Our very own heaven-sent star
You never cease to amaze us
The strength you have is not of this world
You're an angel, a princess, a wonder
And an example of all that is pure

Catriona Toland

11th May

Always Here

When you are so tired that you don't want to speak,
I will help you find the sweetest song.
When your heart beats too fast, enough to scare you,
I will help you breathe the calmest breath.
On mornings when you can't face the world,
I will paint you the most beautiful smile.
Just when you think your tears can't stop,
I will remind you of a fabulous memory that turns the tears to laughter.
And as a scream builds from deep down till you realise you've
Released it, it is loud and it is real
I will hold you in the calm that follows.
Don't you remember me? Do you recognise me?
I am your reason, support, your will.
I am the decision maker, the joker, best friend.
I am the survivor, the solder when you are at war
We are one and the same,
I am you.

Alison Shields

Onomatopoeic Words

Bing, bang, wallop, what a joy to say.
Onomatopoeias you want to use all day.
Ding, dang, dong, just another few.
Example in the dictionary simply is cuckoo.
So many words that originate with sounds.
Stone Age people used them on their hounds.
Started the language that we use today
Expressing exactly what we want to say.

Ann May Wallace

13th May

Without You

I am the gentle rain that falls upon your skin,
Your beauty calls me in your arms of endless love,
Angel wings wrapped round my dove.

I am the rainbow of a crystal sky,
Pastel shades I bring to you,
To paint your life on canvas, new.

I am the call of a mountain stream,
The wolf that echoes through silent night,
An eagle high looking down,
Over distant plains, I can be found,
In the eyes of a buffalo that is white.

I am the wind upon your cheek,
That softly bows within your soul,
To heal the pain and release your chain of old.

All these things and more,
Cannot hide on distant shores,
Drawn by your sun across the sky,
To your land of days gone by,
When you and I could not deny,
Our love so high.

All I am and more is true
But I am nothing without you.

Chris Whooley

Untitled

Spring - gracious spring - bringing new life, new hope
for us all, but also for those who feel they can't cope.
New life - new beginnings from a seed to day's dawn
when the dark days of winter are finally gone.

Fragrant hyacinths, sunny daffodils, they all like to add
to God's glorious spring creation - always happy, never sad.
Majestic magnolia and gentle blossom are included in spring's joy
of this new life, and the hope that we all must enjoy.

I just love it - chill mornings - chill evenings - and the sun of the day -
giving hope to each seedling that summer is on the way.
Take hope from the springtime that life will blossom from now on -
and the dark days of winter are finally gone.

K Windsor

14th May

The Monastery Of Mai-Ling

The lanterns are lit, and the sunset is green,
over the monastery of Mai-Ling!
High; high upon its hill, among
the swooping swallows of spring,
and the bells boom across
the Valley of Sorrows.
And the first twinkling stars
light the sky for our tomorrows!

A Teesdale

Birdsong

When rain comes in like a flood
approaching from the moor,
there is also the song of birds.
Such little feathered things they are,
but messengers of spring.
When birds don't sing
look deep within your heart,
letting your mind be bold,
courageous through the gathering storm,
for they will sing again.

Diana Morcom

New Life

Is anywhere more comforting
Than my garden in the spring?
I watch the flowers unfurling.
I listen to birds that sing.

Troubles in the winter months
Caused anguish and despair;
They fade and seem less harrowing
Because spring is in the air!

So now I look to the future,
Past the season of rebirth;
As Mother Nature heals my wounds -
Pushing new life from the earth!

Brenda Artingstall

Not Alone

When spring arrives we'll wander down, along the river, up the hill
And in the gentle sunshine gaze across the valley green and still.
In summer when the days grow long and dry heat shimmers on the lake
We'll lie in long-grassed fields and hear the birds, the distant song they make
And when the autumn mists set in and haze the woodland silver-grey,
Our muffled steps enshroud within the woody damp of secret days.
Then winter, biting bright and cold and champagne air that chills the soul
When scarves and hats and gloves encase our tingling fingers, glowing face.

Through all the seasons we have walked side by side in light and dark,
In heat and cold and misty haze we've dreamed the nights and lived the days
And never once I've felt alone, although we've wandered paths apart,
Beside me though in body gone, connected always by the heart.
Our lives divide on different plains but golden cords of souls remain,
Linked despite the space and time, though you're not here, you're always mine.

J Johnson

18th May

Thoughts And Observations

Mauve-coloured mountain peaks
With a touch of white upon their brow.
It looks like the weather may soon be grim,
The sky is quite leaden now.

All around me seems very quiet,
Not a lot of activity today,
Splashing torrents of rain now descend
That should keep the vexing gnats away.

All the rushing rain water has made sparkling streams,
The rising mist is now clearing beneath the sun's beams.
On this moor, purple heather, which many insects have found
But after that heavy downpour, few folk are around.

Underfoot - crackling twigs now - and steaming heat
The soaked moor has so quickly begun to dry.
I'm sure there are crickets on the ground
I hear them cheerily singing their cry.

Bees and butterflies in abundance, some birds to be seen,
It's almost as though that downpour had not been.
In daily life we have downpours and irritations abound
But always there's some beauty around to be found.

Muriel I Tate

Happiness

Happiness comes from within.
A little thought provokes a grin,
A happy memory of old
Has kept its thrill when it's recalled.
Sometimes he did, sometimes I'd say
A funny thing that made our day.
The happiness that once we shared
All lives within me unimpaired.

Happiness comes from without.
Some happy laughter or a shout,
To be about on a sunny day
And watch some children at their play.
A chance remark addressed to you
A friendly smile, a 'how'd you do?'
The happiness that others give
Will influence the life I live.

Happiness comes from above.
We don't know why we cry or laugh,
We don't know what the future holds
But take each day as it unfolds.
It's our fate, it's on the cards
We all believe it's in the stars.
My happiness was from Heaven sent
The memory of it will never end.

Lisa Wolfe

19th May

Ode From Swans

Seven white swans with silver wings were flying over a rainbow
A single red rose was at the end of the rainbow, it was wrapped in white satin.
Inside laid a message that read *'I love you'*
One of the swans took the rose in its satin blanket into his beak.
The message inside had to be delivered.
Passing through vanilla-scented clouds and the tips of treetops, we came to a clearing
An angel holding a golden harp stood before us, her hair was like the sun shining upon her face.
Holding out the rose with his silver wings, the angel took hold of the swan's gift
Teardrops began to fall from the swan's tiny eyes, he looked at the angel with such love
She wiped his brown with her delicate fingers
The swan could feel his heart breaking inside of him
His bottom beak began to quiver
She was so beautiful

Emma Bacon

Spring Mist

One spring we strolled by a murmuring stream,
listening to the happy tales it told
of peace and love walking out of a dream
to take their rightful place in a sad world

As we walked, your fingers entwined with mine,
they too with a joyful tale to tell
of lonely gay people thrown a lifeline,
saved from drowning in contempt's ugly swell

We paused, saw two fish in a gentle flow,
wished them safe from the angler's cruel rod,
their colours and grace making a fine show
yet vulnerable, like us, in this world

Crossing a bridge, we paused again and kissed,
peace and love embracing us like spring mist

Roger N Taber

21st May

Speak Only To Sing Love Songs

Gifts of minds to connect,
Colours made by human eyes,
Seeing beneath the skin of the world,
Lifting up objects, but not for gain,
But for help to arrange,
An order to all things,
Pain diminish from joined energy,
Human being and animal united,
That together can share all,
Eat not each other's flesh,
But each other's spirit,
Light is shining, shadow gone,
Speak only to sing love songs.

Jan Bevan

Sunday Complexion

A bright cheerful chrome yellow sun glared
Weightless white clouds
Moved across a brilliant blue sky
Casting pale grey shadows
Over mild green meadows and forest fields
Over high shaded opaque and umber cliffs
The shifting shadows soon disappeared
Where there strongly surged
A magnificent trichromatic ocean
Crashing incessantly upon the shingle shore
Up above gulls circled screeching
Diving down snatched up frightened fish
The gulls looked pleased, looked proud
Some now sit on rocking, rolling waves
Some fly espy cheeky children happily playing
They are running, cheeks both flushed
They are walking every which way
Dogs sniffle, scamper for fun
When chased by the water side
Elderly couples stroll peacefully by
Minding their own private affairs
The ocean crashes upon the wet sandy shore
Sounding like one thousand rifles fired
Against those seaweed covered rocks
Wind blew hard but couldn't equal
The tremendous volume of the sea.

J Flanagan

Love Is ...

Love is the happiness you can't contain
When you remember the times you've shared.
Love is the feeling you can't explain
When you first found out they cared.

Love is the smile you can't help to suppress
When you look into their eyes.
Love is the comfort they always express
When you can do nothing but cry.

Love is the warmth you always sense
When they hold you in their arms.
Love is the belonging, so true, so immense,
The belonging, you know, can't be harmed.

Love is the thing we all live to find,
The meaning in all of our lives.
Love is the gift we dream to be blessed with,
Our partners, our husbands and wives.

Victoria Morley

S nowdrops white
P rimroses bright
R ich beauty spreading
I nto summer heading
N ewness growing
G od overflowing

Marian Bythell

24th May

Safely May You Graze

Safely may you graze
upon grassy meadows green
living in the spring of life,
rather than beneath the chill
of winter's long gloom; instead
that you might know the gentle kiss
of an ocean's soothing breeze,
set across your brow, day in
and day out, amid life's complexities
and the oddities that seemingly lurk,
waiting to pluck at us like a crow
ravaging through an abandoned
picnic lunch.

My friend, safely may you graze
upon grassy meadows green
never forgetting the years I loved
you, incessantly, even
again and again.
Gentle reminders resembling a
serenade of melody; cantatas
swooning over your soul;
filling your heart as no finer
a moment then realised or received,
than the hour you believe in
the power of this love, His love and like a sheep
then graze safely in meadows green.

Carla Iacovetti

25th May

Ascension Day

Our Lord had assembled us, talked to us, sketched out God's plan
For the world He'd redeemed through His love,
His compassion and might.
And He told us, 'That power is to grip you and render you fit
For My work.' Then a cloud fell and took Him right out of our sight.

That power sustained us, inspired us to work with fresh courage
Till we passed in our turn through the clouds to the glory beyond.
And we watched through the ages the clouds
Growing thicker and thicker
As God's love was on offer to Man, and Man failed to respond.

The clouds of unknowing extinguish the road we are treading,
And warring ideas hide the truth in the storm clouds of strife;
While the hurricane Sin robs existence of any real meaning.
We cannot see Jesus, the Way, and the Truth, and the Life.

What a pity Ascension Day's lost its significance for us,
And we fail to remember Christ's friends when His glory drew near.
For 'twas only the eyes of the body were blind to the Saviour -
The eyes of the mind and the soul remained gloriously clear.

Simon Peterson

26th May

We Never Know

We never know, we never know
how long we have in life to go.
We should enjoy all that life brings,
its challenges and happenings.

Delight in flowers, trees and birds,
the beauty of a poet's words,
the lakes, the swans, this country's green,
the magic glow of sunset's scene,
the golden dawn's new day begun,
the chats with friends, laughter and fun,
the pleasure of melodious sound
and comfort felt when homeward bound,
tell of our love, let feelings show
for length of life ... we never know!

Joy Saunders

Nature's Way

Nature's way is fair of hand,
but at times does seem so unkind,
spring is the time of all renewal,
and also the moments of pure despair.
Nature's way is fair of hand,
encouraging, and at times sad,
summer brings warmth from chill,
dry days some, with storms to come.
Nature's way is fair of hand,
sunlight dims, for the cooler thoughts,
autumn brings forth melodic moods,
and slowing is the clock of time.
Nature's way is fair of hand,
crystal-locked, and white with snow,
as winter grips the dormant land,
oh, fair of hand is nature's way.

T D Green

28th May

Before I Disappear

Blow me, blow me up in the sky, life is so dear.
Feel the music, be a tune and then disappear.

Wastes were the years, waste was my ambition, and the world was never kind.
I was guilty! Shame, forget it! Life is calling, oh! never mind.
It's the disco lights and the floors are always thumping.
Be a super star, Oscar nominee, Napoleon, forget the mental dumping.

It's an addiction, it's real; sing loud, happiness was always near.
Feel the music, be a tune and then disappear.

Life is calling, it's going to be a joyride.
Failed; I lost, why the hell I ever tried?
Shame on you for having such a brittle heart which easily broke.
Hey! Wait! Wait! Wait! The previous line was a joke.

Mock the idiots, better forget everybody and let your mind be clear.
Hey! feel the music, be a tune and then disappear.

Sing something! Sing something all along.
Let loose, feel His hand to where you belong.
Put on a smile, step on the gas, do things with your sign.
Feel above everything; feel as if you are on cloud number nine.
This is creation, the sky, ocean and you.
Eat your ice cream before it says, 'Adieu'.

Let your soul free and then with open arm He is calling you near.
Feel the music, be a tune and then disappear.

Divyamaan Srivastava

29th May

To Belong

One born of this world,
Left all, but alone,
Save for the love of a mother and grandmother,
Within the pride, of a family home.

Life's vision often seen,
From the other side,
As the beauty of reflection,
In the crystal flowing waters,
As a portrayal of life.

That given for free,
Of the sharing to be had,
The warmth of the sunlight to own,
The mystery of the darkness,
Revealed by the moonlight,
As the day, draws to a close.

The dawn - at daybreak,
Once again - the calls of the wild,
Unwritten words, spoken - in a chorus of birdsong,
Who could ask for more,
Than of being given the chance,
- To be here -
- To own a place -
And to belong?

Bakewell Burt

Magnificent Splendour

Every morning when I open my eyes
Glancing through the window at blue skies
Listening to the seagulls' cries
Here on my doorstep is a glorious prize.

Strolling, feeling an early morning chill
My whole belonging it seems to fill
Picturesque scenes it seems to instil
These pleasant pastures, making great appeal.

To breathe in the fresh country air
Marvelling at scenery, beautiful and rare
Intoxicated by splendour, drinking my share
Scenic surroundings that are always there.

To behold as streams and rivers flow
Following footsteps to where they go
Climbing mountains, seeing sights below
Absorbing the beauty, my mind will grow.

I can stand on the cliffs gazing out to sea
Watching the vessels as they sail serenely
Invigorated by the views and the tranquillity
That's what my surroundings give to me.

To be able to take in the wonderful sight
Of rare and precious birds as they take flight
Soaring up to such an enormous height
It is a pleasure to express such sheer delight.

Visiting Lake Windermere with awesome views
And be immersed in many glorious hues
Looking around there are so many clues
As to why there's no other place I could choose.

Now I luxuriate in what is all around
Nature's wonder holds me spellbound
Awesome sights in which I am drowned
Peace I sought, I have now found.

B W Ballard

30th May

Among The Empyrean Vortiplanes

Focus on the sky, and the wind flow above
Watch the glint of metal from the wave riders
Always obsessively watch for the byways
Watching for that movement in the weird dimensions
Where increasingly the focus concerns mad space energies
Around those craft, and that flow in the contemplation.

M Courtney Soper

31st May

Timeless

Why is it, I wake up in the morning
nearly always at the beginning of the dawning?
As free as a bird, reflecting on my life,
I'm flying like a kite,
Up and down and round I go,
towards a burning desire
and a promise of a glorified existence.
Smiling, funny, sad, mad.
All the tomorrows hold hope,
yet so many memories to unfold,
to lay out in front and mull over,
don't you see life just baffles me.
From tree to tree,
flower to flower,
house to house,
from cannibals to animals,
to the seven wonders of the world.
A free spirit,
travelled, learned,
Timeless, ageless,
That's me.

M Butcher

Love Can ...

(Dedicated to my wife)

... do wonders for your soul
fill an aching, empty hole
lift your spirits when you're down
make a smile, replace a frown
inspire you when life seems bleak
turn the strongest of knees weak
melt a heart that's made of stone
comfort you when all alone
release your inner light to shine
be that special valentine
ignite the passion and the fire
fan the flames of your desire
make two hearts beat together
be a port in stormy weather
put a spring into your step
give your life that extra pep
soothe the savage beast in man
above all ... love can!

Gary Stephenson

Words Of Kindness

Are like the gentle breeze
upon perspiring skin.
As soothing as a brook on clear crystal days
when long awaited blue heavens
replace all clouds of gloom.

When spoken from the heart
our lips are seasoned with pleasant sound.
Aromatic, uplifting, scented, sweet air
fills an empty void
in a metaphorical way.

So many unkind words are spat forth like venom,
always in a hope of causing emotional injury
and the number seems to grow.

Do not be tearing down.
Instead, be someone who wants to strengthen others.
For even the tiniest of kindness
will outshine all unright.

While letting free these encouragements
upon the ears of those in need
our conscience rewards us.

It does so, because we prove ourselves unselfish
in the giving of good gifts.

Tender kind words at troublesome times
can make a summer sun rise
in winter darkened hearts.

Kevin Welch

3rd June

Nature

See the lilies in the fields
Watch them as they grow
Watch the little snowdrop
As it pushes through the snow
The wonder of the mountains
As they soar towards the sky
The flowing of the river
As it gently passes by
It runs into the ocean
And ripples to the shore
Caressing sandy beaches
With a whisper or a roar
The stars, which fill the heavens
They sparkle and they shine
It's what we know as nature
By the hand known as divine

Grace Divine

4th June

What Makes God Smile?

I'd love to be the reason why
God breaks into a smile.
I want to bring Him pleasure,
Seek to trust Him all the while.

He gets so disappointed when
I fail to heed His voice.
I know He needs my love too
As it makes His heart rejoice.

He always keeps His promises;
Needs me to play a part.
Believing that He knows and
Understands my fearful heart.

He tells me to have faith in Him
He really knows what's best.
It saddens Him when I forget
To put Him to the test.

God needs complete obedience.
Things done without delay.
He shouldn't have to tell me
The reason it's this way.

I'm choosing to obey Him
As He looks down right now.
My first *big chance* to make Him smile,
Please Lord, just show me how!

Gillian Humphries

Chasing The Shadows

The old man relaxes in his chair,
Where yesterday as a child sat there,
And wonders where his life has gone,
Has his memories to look back upon.
He gazes lovingly at his wife,
And for one moment fades the truth,
He sees a young girl sitting there,
Hears the laughter of her youth.
And so as time is slipping by,
Life's pages turning one by one,
He carefully reads each precious line,
And turns some back, to dwell upon.
And so do others tell their tale,
With memory and photographs,
And of tomorrow, what will be?
Froze in time their children's laughs.
And of the old man, what of thee,
Fighting with reality,
Mixed with thoughts of yesterday,
And of tomorrow? Who can say ...

J Brohee

6th June

We Can Do That

A man is building a rainbow.
He uses bricks of strength
and ties them with ropes of hope,
his twinkling eyes setting the curve.

We can do that.
We can roll up our muscles
and build rainbows.

A woman is gathering sunshine,
sprinkling it on the flowers.
The flowers laugh and sing
and throw sunbeams at each other.

We can do that.
We can turn off the dark
and gather sunshine.

Geoff Lowe

7th June

All among the swaggering weeds
a pale protuberance, like a small egg
laid in a little scratched up nest of earth.

That's what I thought it was
and left it there
to be hatched or to be eaten.

And then again I saw it
a little green spike grown
a tuft of comic hair.

Born to the lullaby of garden birds,
watched by the low and hazy sun
and wrapped in dewy mist.

This little miracle
will bloom and be noticed,
will fade and be forgotten.

The cycle will turn around, around
until its small eternity
fades into another greater history.

Fred Brown

8th June

You Will Feel Me

You need never feel alone
For I am always there
I'll never let you down
But forever show I care
You will feel me in the rain
As I drip onto your face
Like little sparks of love
I am trying to embrace
You will feel me in the wind
As I blow right through your hair
And as you feel the chill of it
It will tell you that I'm there
You will feel me in the sun
As my love gives you a glow
My warmth will envelop you
And once again you'll know
I promised to stay near you
And that's just what I'll do
Until that special day arrives
When you will join me too

Margaret Ward

9th June

The Magic Spheres

When a child has been quite good
A special treat is bought -
My favourite gift without a doubt
Gave joy and food for thought.
It was a pot of liquid soap
And a round ring on a stick,
I dipped it in and then I blew -
It was like a magic trick.
A stream of bubbles large and small
Through the ring would fly,
Colourless yet colourful
They drifted up quite high.
Most of them were perfect
Reflecting rainbow light,
Prismatic, diaphanous spheres
Floating out of sight.
But some were slightly wobbly
And exploded with a plop,
They'd formed and flew then disappeared
Stop them - I could not!

Enid Hewitt

Love

Life has brought me an abundance of love
Not riches, pearls or gems
But love the richness of which
Has blessed my life since childhood to old age.
Loving parents and siblings long gone
But whose memories last forever
The bittersweet aura of youth
The freshness may never come again
But I have lived a life full
Of the sense of unfolding magic
Each morning I say a prayer to greet the day
To dedicate my small life to being fully here
And learning how to love
It can only be given and received
It cannot be taken
I am lucky I am loved not for who I am
But for what I am
Love is the hope of the world
The cure for resentment and fear
The one thing that can join nations
And leave Homo sapiens without fear

Phyllis Bowen

11th June

Magic In The Air

Happiness shows in the eyes
As a bumblebee flies
Each day something new
Can brighten the eyes with a view
When night descends
One feels magic in the air
Looking to the sky
Gives a glow to the eye
So many a star
Gives thoughts of rhapsody afar
With heavenly feeling
To send one reeling
With a sense of sanctuary
A land of glory
Then back to earth mind wanders
Filled with wonder
Watching ripples of a stream
Gives the eye a gleam
One feels magic in the air
The mind filled without care
Nothing more can stir the heart
Bringing relaxation ne'er to depart
Thou feel that everywhere
There be magic in the air
So forward thou go
As a stream may flow
With happiness in thy eye
'til the day is nigh

Josephine Foreman

12th June

In these days of troubled times it can be hard to see the good in your fellow man, which is why you must stop for a while and look to the sky and take a deep breath and awaken all your senses.

Awaken your senses to the wonders of this world, the wonder that is you and your life. Remember, you are precious, more valuable than any precious metal known to man.

Being part of the human race can be stressful, tiring and upsetting. We must remember that the human race is exactly that, a race, with every human on the planet.

If you realise this, you will soon understand that we are competing for the same prize.

Love, happiness and good health!

So treat people how you would expect to be treated. Speak to people how you would expect to be spoken to. This will make your race and that of your fellow man a race to enjoy.

Do good to each other and you will surely shine, attracting everyone around you and when they ask why you are so happy, let them know it is because you are part of the most famous race of all time, with a prize money can't buy.

The prize? A long and happy life! The race? The human race!

Live life,
Smile hard,
Do good

The prize is yours ... just take it.

Eugene Dunkley

Lease Lend

And the third world says, 'Lend me your ears
Lend me your arms, your men, your cash.'
Hold that thought, rich western world
Let's not be hasty, let's not be rash
Weren't our ancestors crude and dim
What is more, very, very poor
So we raised our voices to be heard
And together rose to fight tooth and claw
We had pride in our beginnings
Our independence through the years
Gave the right to all the people
A life that's free of doubt or fears
Help alone won't bring you riches
To fight injustice, you must be strong
All your leaders must be honest
There to help you right a wrong
Don't give up the endless struggle
Nurture all the strength within
Though it takes the time of centuries
Strength and God will help you win.

June Davies

14th June

State Of Grace

I am a true citizen of the world,
Living with my sisters and brothers,
Trying to do what the good Lord told us,
Love one another.

For it is simple - why can't you see?
We all came from Adam and Eve, originally,
There should be no borders, we should share the land,
All be helping each other, woman and man.

And there is only one Heaven,
Where we will be free,
And abide together for eternity,
Don't you want to go to this wondrous place?
Live together in a state of grace.

Don't you get sick of the fighting
Scared of the wars?
We should live, by the Lord's commandments,
Not man-made laws.

So try to live in perfection,
Away with bigotry chase,
Live as the Lord pleaded,
In a state of grace.

And when you ask me where I come from,
Judging the colour of my face,
I tell you I'm from every country in the world,
No particular creed or race,

I'm from every country in the world,
And I live in a state of grace.

S Beverly Ruff

15th June

Search For Serenity

Serenity is a word that means peace,
Each one of us should search for inside.
Rest your mind a little and a new life you will lease,
Earnestly look for what you might hide.
Never give up the search for your soul,
Invoke the light that's in you.
Try to see the world as a whole,
Yearn for what you feel to be true.

Christine Blackburn

The Rock Of Christ Is Sure And Strong

Dear God, thank You for being by our side
As a stormy path we had to stride,
You sent Your angels straight from Heaven
When all the prayers for us were given.

We knew the calm of Your still small voice
Which quieten'd our fears so we could rejoice,
Your sustaining power which guided us through
And enabled us to see, all things new.

We felt the comfort of Your Mother Love,
And saw the rainbow in skies above
Promising the sunshine is always near,
The pathway ahead will be bright and clear.

As we journey on, if we should stumble
We know You will not let us crumble
For the rock of Christ is sure and strong,
This is the path You'll carry us along.

Peggy Courteen

16th June

Outlook Changeable

We ask You now, our loving Father God,
Grant peace in spite of threat of war;
Love even in the midst of hate.
These treasured gifts of holy God,
Plant deep within our hearts, we pray, before
We sadly find it is too late
And find our prayers to You above
Not firmly rooted in Your love.

We thank You, Lord, for those who clearly know
Your peace, yes, in the midst of war;
Your love, yes, in the midst of hate.
We pray our lives may also show
These gifts from deep within our hearts before
We sadly find it is too late
And prayers we offer You above
Still hindered by our lack of love.

Elma Heath

Story Time

Just one step
Beyond the front door
There are opportunities
By the score
They may not make one
Rich with fame
As life's a gamble -
It's the name of the game
But if a smile
Perchance one sees
In acknowledged greeting
A stranger may
Become a friend
From just a fleeting meeting.
A host of treasures
May come this way
And who knows what
By the end of day.

Lyn Sandford

My Grandad

I wish you'd known my grandad,
He was so special to me.
After he died, he was replaced
Not by one man, but three!

He cared for a very large park,
With walled garden and potting shed,
Lawns that stretched forever,
With shrubberies, trees and flower bed.

Then down the wide stone steps
The Dell - a place of mystery, in shade.
Rustling bamboos fringed a still, dark pool,
Stony paths wove a way to quiet glade.

Grandad tended all of this
As if it were his own;
But Sundays, he always kept for chapel,
Through his example -
The seeds of my own faith were sown.

I wish you'd known my grandad!

Jean McPherson

On Top Of The World

(Dedicated to all my family and friends who keep me smiling!)

I'm on top of the world
For everyone to see,
I can't quite believe that
This feeling's inside me.
Waiting to erupt
Climbing more and more,
Until my feet are no longer
In contact with the floor.
I feel an emotion
That words can't convey,
An exuberance, excitement,
A feeling so gay!
I feel like I want
To shout it out
To leap with joy
And dance about!
There are such beautiful things
That I want to take in,
Amazing sights that
Leave me with an awe-struck grin!
I love this feeling
That makes life worthwhile
As when I feel on top of the world
I can't help but laugh and smile!

Sarah Stephenson (16)

20th June

Today

Although our yesterdays
Live on today
Remembering, often
What we might say
And, as each new day
Breaks precious dreams,
We pause and sigh and then
Realise, it seems
Today will be yesterday, tomorrow
Yet we cope
Somehow we continue and
Wish and hope.

Pauline Pickin

Daily Reflections

What do we know about today?
Now's a fleeting moment
And today is the afterlife
Or reincarnation of yesterday.
It is also the preconception of tomorrow.
All days and nights consist of time
Which is immortal.
E'en though there is an end
To our physical time,
Eternity proceeds and we are
Immeasurably part of it.
So living for today takes care
Of all our yesterdays
And then allows certainty of a secure future.

D W Hill

Unforeseen Problem

An unforeseen problem that shouldn't be there
If you find that you have one please do not despair
For all of these troubles come out from the mire
Eventually ridding you of this hot burning fire

Complete understanding and comparative thought
Tends to make this such a damning resort
So just do as you will and feel soul within
Life is too short so now we must all begin

Where was the problem we have really forgot
We look down inside us, therefore we must not
Relinquish the horror that makes this thing yearn
Like healing again and maybe someday we'll learn.

Steve Matthews

23rd June

A Windy Summer's Day With My Daughters, Catherine And Lucy

The sun comes out at intervals
As the clouds race quickly by
The sea tones in with Cornish rocks
Turning slate grey to white, windy froth,
As one set of footprint goes down the dune
Onto the virgin, damp sea-wet sand
And then another set follows
I follow on with my footprints
Behind my daughters' prints across the beach.

Off we three go around the headland
Past the tamarisks to Polly Joke beach
The wind is whirling and very strong
It tests its strength against my form
And pushing, so very nearly wins!
In a circle, walking we go
Red poppies flop to and fro
Golden corn marigolds shake and tremble
His power and force can be so strong
But God surely makes these cornfield flowers
Able to stand the Cornish wind's force
That even man finds hard to endure ...
A testing strength of His great might
But, like the footprints on the sand,
God shows us all His loving care
That He will carry us through trials and stress
Until we can face the winds again.

Anne Veronica Tisley

24th June

Believe In Yourself

B elieve you can do anything you
E ver wanted to do!
L ive your life to the fullest!
I nvite the unexpected in. Do not
E ject from your thoughts what is the
V ery passion in your heart.
E mbrace life! Not death!

I nvest time in yourself.
N ever give up!

Y ou will find the peace
O nly you have to try to
U nderstand the pressures of life.
R ealise that times can be tough.
S tick with it!
E verything will come right in the end.
L ook after yourself. Learn to live and be
F ree!

Rosie Heartland

25th June

Love You

The way ahead may look so long with no real end in sight,
however bleak the outlook seems remember there is light.
The old clichés come pouring out; 'well-meaners' stop to say,
'At least it can't get any worse.'
Get lost, you think, not say!

Whatever life has thrown at you, you took it on the chin,
so if you'll just bear with me now, that's where I will begin.
With heart of gold and mind so strong, you jumped the train of life,
imagining the stations, but not expecting strife.

Each trial that came to test you brought strength and knowledge too,
but then one day the train pulls up at 'God, what do I do'?
It chips away your spirit, devours your zest for living,
till one day you're admitting that you just can't go on giving.

It all appears too much to bear, a mountain you can't climb,
yet simple as this maybe sounds, 'self love' and lots of time.
Get back to who you really are and things that make you smile,
try to give something to 'you' each day, for just a while.

We make our own worst nightmares then trap them in our head,
instead of resting peacefully the demons rear instead.
The thoughts we think are ours alone; there's no one else in charge
we take our little problems and we 'think' them very large.

We hear too many voices, they dictate who we should be,
but tuning to the voice inside will really set us free.
So as you wake tomorrow, be good to you and say,
'I'm such a special person and I love me just this way.'

Fiona Geelan

Friendly Advice

Kind words that are never spoken
Good deeds that are left undone
Leave memories only of regret
For days that are now long gone

Always think most positive
In all the things you do
Dreams you have for the future
Will then someday come true

What fills a heart with gladness
And makes the day worthwhile
Troubles seem to disappear
When you're greeted by a smile

Memories shared with loved ones
With the laughter and the tears
Will be your greatest treasure
Through all the future years.

Shirley Gwynne

26th June

Mr John Andrews Dedication

As you dedicate your life anew
May God, go with you, in all you do
Whatever path your feet may tread
May God be always, at your head
Whatever task, you may pursue
Love, faith and trust, stay with you
God's wondrous love, will see it through
His ever open arms, will lead you on
From strength to strength, until day is done
Until the evening shadows fall
His love will keep you safe, until the morn
To lead your flock, free and from harm.

Irene Corbett

27th June

A Country Meadow

Strolling through,
The country meadow,
On a hot summer's day,
The sweet, sweet scent,
Of honeysuckle,
Perfumes the air,
Over the sty
And down by the creek,
I slowly,
Make my way.

Cows grazing contentedly,
In a distant field,
The humming of a bumblebee,
Brings music to my ear,
I stop,
At the old stone bridge,
To have a rest,
Watching,
Listening,
To the sound,
Of the water,
Trickle by.

Carole Herron

27th June

Waiting For Our Tomorrow

Constantly on my mind
Thinking of all the things we've yet to do
Of the times we'll come to share
How I wish that tomorrow was here

And although from me you're far away
Just the thought of you makes me smile
And helps me get through the everlasting day
When tomorrow seems too far out of reach

But one day soon tomorrow will be today
When our waiting will be over
And I'll have you by my side
Holding me through the night

But then tomorrow will become yesterday
And again I must wait for tomorrow to come around once more
But I'm not looking for an intervention
Because I know I want and love you so

So until our next tomorrow
I remind myself of our yesterdays
Trusting in the knowledge that the sun will rise again
And that your heart will always lead you back to me.

Elaine Donaldson

For Mother

God saw her birth.
He knew her days.
He knew her.
A child who grew
from innocence to stature,
though ever chasing
mind dreams, still,
half ground, half sky.

And marriage came
and with it threefold children:
her cherubim
and sole dream.
And how she loved
and loves us still,
this Earth-born angel
sent to bless:
appeaser.

A teacher,
a wife,
a saint,
a mother,
a silent sufferer.

Diamond heart,
gentle rock.
Poppycock.
Her life
a maze of school and pets and meetings.

I am indebted.
You are imperative to me.

Caroline Baker

My Happy Place

I love this place, my homeland
I love its rolling hills
Its flowers and trees and valleys
Its dancing brooks and rills.

I love the shady woodlands
Where cheeky robin sings
And buzzards glide high overhead
On swift, but silent wings.

I love its leafy tunnels
Through beechwoods bright and new
The pools of dappled sunlight
And blue sky peeping through.

I wander through green meadows
Where honeysuckle grows
And buttercups and cowslips
And clouds of wild rose.

With age my love and longing
For my happy place increase
It's here I find tranquillity
True beauty and deep peace.

Estelle James

Life Happens

(God is there)

No matter who we are,
Or what our lifestyle holds,
The bible tells us clearly
The love of God enfolds.
Sometimes we find it hard
Believing what we read,
The promise of God's presence
Seems not to meet our need.
But we must remember
We share God's world on Earth,
With all of His creation ...
Know life for what it's worth.

No matter who we are
Life 'happens' day by day
To all who walk upon this Earth,
That's when we need to pray.
For life's blows may hurt us,
Life's trials come our way.
Our dreams may 'crash' before us
And troubles take full sway.
But God will *never* leave us,
His promises are sure.
When life 'happens', He is there,
Our lives in Him secure.

No matter who we are
We have a God who cares,
Who treasures and protects us ...
(His love comes unawares)
So we must learn to trust,
Believing in His word
That He will never leave us,
We have His message heard.
And so as life just 'happens'
To me, as well as you,
Remember, God *is* with us
To share in all we do.

Anne Gray

30th June

Through light I can reach a place
where no trace of thought remains
where 'we' and 'I' can discover the canvas of existence
defuse notions being forgotten and left behind

through light I can reach that place
where feelings and emotion upwell to explode
to where starbursts illuminate the pathways
and there the journey leads to 'home'

through light wholeness of me and of experiences felt
where body and soul in rapture entwine
where pleasures soar on ephemeral zephyred breezes
blown softly as eider through space and time

through light I see my oneness
where within a flash of dazzling brilliance I exist
there to be joined by the soulmate 'she'
inspired to thence shine as a co-joined guiding star

through light ...
may you ...
walk ...
grow ...
feel ...
sense . . .
and ... oh yes ... love

Michael Boase

30th June

The Church At Hodnet

A stone face tombstone, weather worn, records the lives of those long gone
In a churchyard where the grass is shorn by sheep as close as any lawn
Seen in the nearby stately pile, inducing me to stay awhile
Perchance my forebears trod that isle and worshipped in the olden style
An artisan who gave his faith and brought his son into this place
For clergy to anoint with grace the holy water to the face.
Of the infant who in time would leave the village in his prime
To join the soldiers of the line, fighting in the mud and grime
For King and Country in a warn two score miles past Flanders' shore
Which they were told some weeks before would be the war to end all war
It didn't seem so in this Hell, when suddenly the rivals' shell
Dislodged him from his horse, he fell and although hurt, he bade farewell,
Emotions high but well concealed, to the horrors of that battlefield
Then given time his wounds were healed, through past events his future sealed
A country fit for heroes, his sights were set so high,
Never would he toil again beneath that rural sky.
Business in the city for the remainder of his days,
He gave his life to commerce he learned their urban ways
He bought a house; he took a wife, he found investment pays,
He lived a comfortable life, his parents were amazed
And as the last millennium drew swiftly to its end
He left this life, his family, his home and all his friends,
Those active in that conflict could never comprehend,
A life so long and fruitful as no one would portend.
Standing by that self same church, a century on in time,
Searching for the family of that relative of mine
I feel a warmth, an inner peace and think it may define
A basic need in people, who with passing years refine,
Their goals, their aspirations, a ladder there to climb,
Yet all along the simple life to everyone is prime.

John Harrison

1st July

Colour Palette

The vaulted sky may change its hue
It encircles the Earth, both me and you
Fiery orange, red, cream or grey
Or dark by night and blue by day.

As we gaze up to the skies above
It feels we are enveloped by love
The Lord above knows how you feel
He has the power to bless and heal.

Penny Miller

Phoenix Of The Soul

Flames flicker in the dark of night,
distant stars shine tranquil bright,
warm glow pervades the sight
an entrancing subtle light.

Fiery dance shall draw you deep
capture like hypnotic sleep.
Spirit shines as salamanders leap,
vision swirls, a message to keep.

Sacred wood burns
ancient blood rises, turns,
heart fire calls, yearns,
phoenix of the soul transforms, learns.

Sharon Townsend

The Solitary Lemon Tree

The lemon tree has grown here,
For many a long year.
Sprung from a discarded pip,
From someone's cocktail drink,
Which had diligently sprouted,
Betwixt the time-worn cobbles,
In this ancient courtyard.
Identified early as not a weed,
Endured and in due course flowered.
Its richly scented blooms delightful.
The tiny fruit initially uninspiring,
As green as its glossy leaves,
Then growing, slowly changing,
To its familiar shape and colour,
Such an acrid, primary yellow.
Its taste then sharp and pleasant.
The branches filling out and spilling,
Over the white-washed, courtyard wall.
Ten feet tall, evergreen and sprawling,
And thus, in a passageway I saw it,
One hot and sunny July morning,
In the enchanting town of Port Christo,
On the beautiful isle of Majorca,
Close to the acclaimed Caves of Drach.
Some thirty years having passed,
And there, for all I know, it still grows.
It was oblivious to my admiration.
Snared in the weft and warp of my life,
Which I still relish with much delight.

Julia Pegg

2nd July

Carrying On

No warning came, left alone
Sadly to mourn, emotionally lame.
My love gifted his last breath to me,
Simply slipped away, left me
Urging, I should carry on,
Saying, he knew I would.
Much I did cry and wished to die.
But remembering my promise,
Sought to try, ceased piping my eye.

From duty, we should not shift,
For life lent is but a gift; decision made to
Make the grade, felt at once, my heart lift
Death had made a rift, which may never heal,
Yet the future must not steal
Make new beginnings,
Hold your crease, for a good innings
That umpire in the sky bids you try.
He, at last judgement will ask you why
Why you missed your chance to
'Slow Dance', pausing to look upon your way,
For unfortunate people having
A kind word to say.

If only passing the time of day.
Music of life does not forever play
Advising them too, those
Simple things to do; take time
To stop and stare, smell the flowers
Good times we share
In sunshine and showers.

Graham Watkins

3rd July

Summertime Blessings

When the magic of spring
has danced her dance,
and the sweetness of summer
is here at last,
I shut my eyes
and listen to nature's business of the day.
I hear the hum of the bees,
as they collect pollen and nectar from the flowers.
Sweet music floats down from the trees in birdsong.
I can feel the passing breeze stroking my face,
and I love to smell the sweet perfume from the lilies and the roses.
The blue lavender gives off its aromatic smell as I walk past.
The sun shining down from a clear blue sky,
reflects a rainbow of colours from the flowers,
each one being unique.
The smell of the newly mown grass hangs in the air.
I love watching butterflies
silently glide across the garden.
As they gently land on the flowers to feed on the nectar,
they fold their wings together, sealing the artist's work within.
When they have finished feeding,
they bathe in the sunlight
revealing the creator's painting with open wings.

There are so many wonderful things to enjoy in the summertime.

Linda Knight

My Plea

Be with me in the morning, Lord,
Be with me in the day,
Be with me all my life, Lord,
Please be here to stay,
I want You in my life, Lord,
I want You here to stay.

Deirdre Wise

Two Sights

We open our eyes for visions of planet Earth
A child crying, joining us the first day of birth
Persons passing, smiles on their faces, talking
To maybe a loved one, arm in arm walking
Colours of all kinds blending our sight
From early morning to late dusk at night
Patterns of things as they pass our way
As the hours tick along the hourly day
Yet we see what should never be seen
Where evil is black and never grass green
Wars of red blood, people never seeing again
Who lived a life but not time of age to gain
Man, woman and child who wanted only life
Part of a majority who meet strive
Ones only rich in feelings and thought
Who work, parents, teachers taught
To love their neighbour as themselves
Yet exist the evil ones that delve
Into sins that should never be seen
Their minds corrupt, many years been
To close your eyes to such can be done
But would this war of sins be ever won?
That make those we see laughing die
Bringing sorrow and tears to the eye
Can our sights make peace be bought
By making those that are evil be taught
That they see by sight good around
Splendour of nature and humans found
Blue skies, green fields, people living
To their planet Earth returns giving
To be born living their life's span
Unspoilt by any other living human

Brian Frost

Beyond

Sea road, the wind at your back, leaves twigs sand,
a flow of scurrying things overtakes you
on tracks like strings shot into the horizon.
Grey-lilac clouds run and behind them the sun
lights up a spot, inflames it, comes out
and for an instant blinds you:
three hundred and sixty degrees of world
catch you up in a silent clap,
you breathe, take the vastness in and sense
more days like this to come, and more horizon
beyond this breath of yours, this flow,
this is the happiness you know.

Davide Trame

6th July

Moments

A rickety road,
A harmonious island.
This concoction forms:

Hazy summer scents
Caress the tranquil island.
Encompasses you.

Streaks of amber flash.
Effulgent sun in mid-sky.
Intensifying.

Silent sea. Stillness.
A sapphire silk blanket.
All movement suppressed.

Nature awakens.
Creatures meet. Murmur content.
Constant melody.

Sun bids soft goodnight,
Frames island in silhouette;
Casts purple shadows.

Focus disarrayed.
Countless moments blur to one;
Lulled asleep slowly.

See, hear, smell, taste, feel.
A snippet. A slice of life.
Absorb each moment.

Emily Thommes

6th July

Rolling Along Past

Rolling along past ...
  a stream snaking through the dense growth,
  water rippling over stones,
  leaves rustling in the wind.
Rolling along past ...
  cast off boxes and bins,
  lumber and asphalt,
  mattresses and luggage.
Rolling along past ...
  unused siding, forgotten box car
  parked by abandoned loading docks,
  an age gone by.
Rolling along past ...
  back doors and swimming pools,
  barbecues and bicycles,
  exposed to the rolling voyeurs.
Rolling along past ...
  a vacant lot soaked in swampy water,
  a hidden world of frogs and rats,
  and mosquitoes as large as a toenail.
Rolling along past ...
  a power transformer, coils and cables and trestles,
  the visible of invisible flow,
  lighting up and carrying along.
Rolling along past ...
  until I get off, step down,
  walk to the front,
  and enter into the moving crowd.

John A Mills

7th July

Alchemy

When in my mind I balance all my woes
against the joy that from your brightness springs,
and weigh the heavy weight that with them goes
against the lightness your dear presence brings;
and when in your expressive eyes a tear,
softening laughter, takes compassion's part,
and in the mischief of your voice I hear
the gentle music of your playful heart -
oh then (strange alchemy!) your lightness turns
the scale of worldly values upside down;
all debts diminish and dull care adjourns
when subject to the sway of your bright crown:
if wealth be marked by weight when it is told,
your lightest glance of love were heaviest gold.

Bernard Brown

7th July

Why You're So Special

(Dedicated to the loving memories of strong hands that kept me safe and secure, and the pitter-patter of tiny feet and to old friends whose wisdom will outlive them)

Why you're so special to me:
You're never judgmental yet firm to the point
You embrace me with words that heal me, tender and kind
You empower my broken mind so I become whole and bold.
You're always ready to listen, you motivate me,
With you I feel ready to fly and if I should trip and fall
You'd dust me off and say, 'Stand tall.'
There were times I could have given up,
But just the thought of you reminds me
That I have already won the battle, breaking the shackle.
Your empathy is beyond compare
Your grace and beauty is truly rare;
I'm taken aback, your love is overwhelming
I can't help yearning for another day with you;
Where I can be myself having no need for pretending.
So let me take this time to let you know,
My life without you would be like a bed of roses
That refuses to grow.

Norma Jean Johnson

A Prayer For The Living (A New Day Will Dawn)

Throughout the darkest night
With no more strength to fight
When lives are tossed and torn
A new day will dawn

When lights at tunnel's end
Out of sight around the bend
The path winds on and on
A new day will dawn

When loves are lost and won
With some things left undone
And sadness falls forlorn
A new day will dawn

When siblings cause the hurt
Rub noses in the dirt
Their lives keep moving on
A new day will dawn

When no one seems to care
People stand and stare
Pass judgement with a scorn
A new day will dawn

When you feel dire dread
With some words left unsaid
You'll keep holding on
A new day will dawn

Your spirits are so low
And nowhere else to go
The piper blows his horn
A new day will dawn

With problems magnified
And all the nights you cried
You'll wake and sense the morn
A new day has dawned

P Ellis

Thoughts

I sat upon my garden seat
One sunny afternoon,
The flowers bloomed all around me,
Bird songs were all in tune.

The warmth of the sunshine
And the gentle wafting breeze,
Made me feel contented,
An my heart was so at ease.

My eyes took in the beauty
Of a lovely pansy face,
How great was our Creator
To make a world so full of grace.

Thoughts tumbled through my mind,
As I sat there all forlorn,
It made me wish the world would change
And we could be reborn.

This would make us think again,
To try with all our might
To make the world a better place
And put all things to right.

To love, not hate; be kind, not cruel,
All selfishness to cease.
In every way the whole wide world
Would learn to live in peace.

So look around you every day,
Thank God for so much pleasure,
And try to do your little bit
To live up to His measure.

Margaret Findlay

9th July

Be Thankful

You think that you are unlucky
But there are lots worse than me
Some have never seen the blue sky
None have ever seen the sea
And there are birds that fly
Some have never walked or talked
And never seen the fields of green
Some have never been out of their beds.
So if you've got your eyes to see
Can see the wonder of nature
Can see the high mountains
And the tall trees
Just say a prayer for those who cannot see
And thank the Lord that He makes us well again.

H W Gosling

Highers

H appy that exams are over for now
I ndeed the learning, swotting, and sweat on one's brow
G reat expectations, the waiting, then *wow!*
H opefully top marks; if not, try again
E very student's ability, put to the test now
R ealising dreams, and fruition for some
S hows in the end, hard work has to be done.

Sheila Macdonald

11th July

Something Greater Than Ourselves

Shall we let today be the first true footstep
Along the path towards tomorrow's journey?

Shall we hold ourselves to the promise of a brighter future
For every single neighbour, near and far?

Shall we temper our demands for human rights
With responsibilities and social equity?

Shall we set aside mere thoughts of self-indulgence
For real action on the hunger of our fellow man?

Shall we forego ownership and speak instead of tending
As passing stewards of our children's children's home?

Shall we reach out to lead the narrow minds of warfare
To a focus on the broader visions spread across the sky?

Shall we join our hands and work together
For the aim of something greater than ourselves?

David Gasking

The Pathway

Choose in life the tranquil path
paved with peace, devoid of wrath
where every gentle woman and man
love makes welcome, hate does ban.
Once found - you can never stray
from the quiet tenor of its way.

Great your burden, heavy the load;
weightless it feels upon that road
where briar, thorns and bramble
give way before you as you ramble
along a route of stingless nettle
and calm and joy upon you settle ...

Dispelling sadness, soothing pain
cooling your ire as gentle rain.
They who would this pathway find
are those who caring ever mind
their neighbour known or strange
through all this worldly range.

Dry your tears, greet the smile
bravely face each yearly mile;
be calm, be kind and you will never lose
sight of the pathway that you must choose.

Anthony J Brady

12th July

Morocco Bound

Her singing is a tonic for the old,
upon her laughing face they thrive,
she is my daughter blessed with heart of gold,
her voice elixir to revive
the languishing but now she's weary too,
despite the smile that lightens hearts;
and so she travels, wings to pastures new,
into refreshment's realm departs.
Visions of her enchanted smile prevail,
measuring paths of blue mystique;
acquisitive ascent to dreams grows pale,
upon return I know she'll speak,
elaborate on buildings blanched by light,
diffused by solar beam of gilt
and desert sands ethereal by night;
traders' uninterrupted lilt.
The elderly she loves confer,
confused on dates she'll entertain,
they know that they can count on her
when she, renewed, comes home again.
Shall song be tinted by the east
and an alien warmth transmit
its fire, pure eloquence increased,
my angel's eyes by secret lit?

Ruth Daviat

12th July

God in 'all'
in all I see,
Thou who changest not
change me
to be what Thou wants me
to ... 'be'.

ADMT

The Encounter

Lord, look upon me
Inward, outward let me be
Open, warm, loving - free
To lead that self-giving life
Protected in the spiritual strife.
Descend upon me, as a dove
Fill me full of Jesus' love.

Brian Strand

My Saviour

My Saviour of time
Is it You I will find?
When I kneel and pay homage to Thee.
Or will Heaven deny
Take these tears that I cry
And then offer them up so You see.
That I am now broken
These words rarely spoken
Hence my heart whispers prayers from within.
My life I can't give
For each moment I live
I pray You hold forgiveness of sin.
So what do I do
If my soul turns from You
And this presence I fear does encroach?
For if I'm alone
In this darkness unknown
Then this Hell I despise will approach.
Yet now as I speak
I feel love so complete
Lifting doubt and despair from this grave.
Whilst angels surround
Once again I am found
Through Your silence my life You have saved!

James Michael Thomas

The Garden Of Life

Life is like a garden
Just let me explain -
It has to be re-seeded
For things to grow again.

The weeds they come to balk us
To put pitfalls in our way
But then we overcome them
As we do so every day.

The flowers are our children
Nurtured by love and care
Each one we find is different
But some are very rare.

The birds nesting in the treetops
Caring for their young
Remind us of our parents
Whose good works go unsung.

Grandfather is the oak tree
Standing so firm and strong
He's a shoulder there to cry on
When you know you have done wrong.

Rain falls in the garden
It reminds us of Grandmother
As this lady washes fears away
For she loves us like no other.

We could go on forever
But I think it's safe to say
Whatever's in the garden
Will never go away.

Barbara Finch

15th July

Our Future Together

Know I dream about you all of the time,
Wonder what will happen to you and me.
Suppose I must be patient, wait let be,
But I hope that one day you become mine.
Being apart's such a terrible bind,
Perhaps we could move, live beside the sea.
Wish we could always be as one, I love thee,
Sure that as a couple we would be fine.

I can only function when you are near,
Best when my head's upon your shoulder laid.
For when you are close by I know no fear,
Loud music on the stereo will be played.
Some words of love are what I long to hear,
Plans for future together will be made.

S Mullinger

16th July

A Special Love

My angel's gone to Heaven
Last night she said goodbye.
She gently kissed my forehead
As in my bed I lie.
She knew my heart was aching
So tried to ease the pain,
Reassuring my troubled thoughts
That we will meet again.
But my heart is still so heavy,
It feels it never will recover,
For I miss that special love
That grows between a daughter and her mother.

Marlene Parmenter

The Pearl

(A triolet)

Each heart knows its own sorrows and stings
But no stranger takes its pearl of joy
Our troubles and delights wring and sing.
Each heart knows its own sorrows and stings
But from God's love confidence springs
His fellowship is without alloy.
Each heart knows its own sorrows and stings
But no stranger takes its pearl of joy.

Derek Norris

17th July

Sharing

Father, Son and Holy Ghost - a perfect paradigm
of sharing life and love that's shared, eternally entwined.
No loneliness in this oneness as nothing is withheld
so each is fully each and other, joyous in the meld.
This overwhelming love floods out and will not be contained.
It is creation's life and joy and Heaven's one refrain.
So were we made, to love and share, one body and one bread,
sent out in power from Mother Church by Christ, Her Lord and Head.

Linda Barnard

Poetic Inspiration

Poetry comes from the heart,
It communicates simple truths,
And concepts that are difficult
To understand.

Accessible to young and old,
To every race and creed,
It is worth its weight in gold,
Bringing hope to those in need.

Poetry can be divinely inspired,
Opening your eyes,
Lifting your spirits to greater heights,
Helping you see things in a new light!

Cathy Mearman

Welcome This Day

When thunder threatens
think of sun.
Scotch troubles before
they have begun.
Wipe the frown
from off your face,
then put a smile
back in its place.
Disregard that
snide remark;
let light come in
when it seems dark.
Set your worries
on one side,
come into the open
do not hide.

So all in all
have a lovely day -
forget the work,
just go out and play!

Joyce Hockley

Contrail At Sunset

Trapped in ice crystals, a trailing rainbow
at thirty thousand feet tracks a Boeing,
gliding like an invisible dot, so
high it sails. The moving spectrum's snowing
gold, crimson, bronze calligraphy as clouds
of cotton in a vast accumulation
pile up their plump, white pillows, each endowed
with nimbuses and grandeur of creation.
As pipistrelles skim and swallows dart,
a sussurus riffles across the grass,
knocks at my soul and penetrates my heart.
I feel its gentle murmur stir and pass.
Now hushed, at peace, hangs the whole world of nature
with, scrawled across the sky, God's signature.

Norman Bissett

20th July

The Way

The world is in a shaky state
Of famine, war and strife,
We should unite together
To ensure a better life.

Each dawning as the light appears
It brings a glimpse of hope
To every person in the world,
Helping them to cope.

The famine has to cease,
Food it must be shared
Around the poorest in the world,
To show them that we cared.

The bombs must stop dropping,
Innocent people die,
Help to build a world of peace,
Everyone must try.

Bombers in trains and buses,
Trained to maim and kill,
Must be re-educated
To help to do God's will.

Let us live together,
In laughter, joy and love,
To help each other daily,
The way to Heaven above.

E M Gough

20th July

The Love Of God

The love of God is an extraordinary
And a superlative life force.
Influencing men and women to pray and serve
Beyond natural willingness and capacities.
It is an irresistible nutrient for hungry souls;
A necessity for stability and
The well-being of life,
And an essential resource
For harmonious relationships.

The love of God clothes with true dignity;
Covering faults and failings;
Esteeming the lowly,
Accepting the unlovely and forgiving offences.
Motivating the virtuous,
And stirring the merciful to compassionate deeds.

Those influenced by the
Excelling attributes of His love,
Are the ones who become
Exemplars in His love.
Therefore be willing and aspire always
To receive the love of God
In Christ Jesus our Lord.
So that from the springs of His love,
May emanate all that you may seek to do.
Hallelujah.

Azariah Ephratah

Patience

How oft have I a letter written,
To one who has my senses smitten;
Pouring out in wrathful phrase
Writing through an angry haze,
Words with bitter acid drip,
Spurning decent penmanship;
Anxious only to give back
Hurt for hurt, black for black!

Then overnight through sleep's calm waves,
Anger's storm no longer raves;
Yesterday's ire seems less intensive
Yesterday's hurt seems less offensive;
Re-read the letter, modify it
Will that phrase do? Well then, let's try it
Should I state with such malignity
Or maintain a quiet dignity?

Humour returns, so with a grin
My letter ends up in the bin;
The moral of this little rhyme,
If you are hurt at any time
By insults real or unintended,
Before you feel too much offended
And jump in kicking with both feet,
Wait 'til you've had a good night's sleep!

N Ferguson

Junkie

Life is a drug I cannot quit
Or even try to regulate
Regardless of its side effects
That leave me in a frenzied state,
For life's a necessary trip
That seldom beckons censorship.

I need a daily fix of life
And all of its reality
To keep my spirit kicking in
From now until eternity,
And should cold turkey rear its head
I'll take a dose of life instead.

I get my kicks from life itself
Because I'm hooked incessantly
By its intensifying buzz
That oozes with sheer ecstasy,
And every addict knows fine well
That life can put an end to Hell.

Life is the safest trip I know
That keeps me ever-pacified
And I can openly confess
Its use has kept me satisfied,
For life's a drug I cannot quit
And not a pill can challenge it.

Iaian W Wade

22nd July

I Will Follow You

I will follow You
Until the ends of the Earth
Then I'll sing aloud
Of Your praise and glory
I will follow You
Until my life is over
Until I die
And I meet You in Heaven
I will walk Your path
And keep You close to my heart
Then I'll stand aside
And revel in Your glory

I will follow You
Meet You all the way
Cherish the Earth that You tread
Marvel at Your every word
Sing to the Lord
Sing of His redemption
Praise Him on high
Praise every day for His breath
I will follow You
End up in Heaven on high
Until life is over
And my new one begins
I will follow You
Dear Lord
I will follow You

Elaine Day

23rd July

A New Dawn

Honour and devotion
Lives in every emotion
So no matter who you are
A new dawn waits from afar
One voice in jubilation
Pure blessings for salvation
For a precious gift of life
A new dawn shines so bright

A new dawn with comfort and peace
The presence of love on every street
The Lord God will embrace you so
As a new dawn begins to grow

There is nothing to fear
When God is near
He'll conquer evil and sin
As a new dawn waits within
With Heaven in your heart
God will play a part
Faith lifts you with elation
To a new dawn of creation

Frank Howarth-Hynes

24th July

How Odd Of God!

Oh God, are You for English men
of rather noble line,
who look divine,
whose manners are so fine?

And are You, God for Scotsmen bluff
who do good work,
who never shirk
and always go to kirk?

And do You favour, God
that man from Wales
who preaches in the vales,
whose congregation quails?

God said, 'I am for women and,
come to that, for men like you, dear boy,
who talk to Me from time to time.
It needn't even be in rhyme!'

Peter Davies

25th July

God Be With Me (My Prayer)

God be my strength and Saviour
When troubles may be near,
God be my guidance with Your light
And guide me through my fear.

God be within my healing hands,
To free others from their pain,
That through Your understanding and Your help,
They will feel well again.

God help them to feel they are not alone,
And show them that You care,
Teach them to speak to the Lord above,
As their problems they will share.

And through Your love and guidance,
Please give them hope that they
Will feel the power of perfect peace,
And will get stronger every day.

So Lord, please be in my mind today
And tell me the exact words that I must say,
Help me to help others who are too blind,
That through Your understanding, You will bring peace of mind.

Barbara Holme

The Gift Of Life

You're the blood from my veins
You're the beat of my heart
You're the tears in my eyes
You're the breath in my lungs

I gave you the gift of life
I gave you the strength to live
I gave you the sight to see
I gave you a little of me

When you feel pain, I cry with you
When you feel joy, I laugh along too
When you feel fear, I feel it too
When you feel anxious, I worry too

We are but one
My children and I
Everything they are is a little of me
Everything I am is a part of them

Tracie Rhodes

27th July

From Wilderness To Promised Land!

From wilderness to Promised Land.
From darkness into light.
From grief and pain -
To joy and healing -
You'll lead us precious Lord.
If we but come to You
And take Your outstretched hand,
Follow on Your pathway
Walking close to You!
For You promised, dearest Lord,
That when we come to You
We will find true rest and peace -
Together Lord with You!
Our burden's light -
For Holy one -
You bear them all with us!

Christina Miller

Invitation

We will get you in the end my friend,
It is time all people of this world, their ignorant ways amend.
This special message of importance with love we send,
Wake up, listen, heed and all will apprehend.
The magic of love, compassion, wisdom and truth,
In order to obtain the golden key of eternal youth.

Unite with us now, our invitation extends to one and all,
And respond with diligence and humility to our universal call.
Lift up your eyes, open your hearts, true revelation will be your reward,
To a new beginning, sisters and brothers of peaceful moral accord.

Patricia Rose Thompson

28th July

Enchantment Today

An amazing bird's eye view, I see, of a garden set before me,
So fresh and green the lawn, so bright and splendid the bee
Descending gracefully on the radiant, colourful flowers
Setting itself on the leaves, amid overall splendour in the bowers.

The pearly white roses are expanding in glorious array,
Deliciously pink hydrangeas with flowers closely bound on display
Deep red geraniums, clustered and to attention stand,
While a mixed assortment of bright orange and lemon marigolds blend.

Clematis is slowly, gracefully, climbing the green frame
Bursting forth, in fits and starts, like a beautiful purple flame,
Beneath the frame, the spotted, yellow pansies sit astride
The earth, spreading out in clusters, languishing with pride.

This formation, resembling a symmetry of contrasting colours,
Expresses the dazzling, elegant, enchantment and contour
Of beauty, lustrous enrapture, amid an aroma of relaxing, scented air,
Which I perceive, in this bird's eye view glimpse of a garden,
Brought forth with loving tender care.

Phyllis Wright

29th July

Help Is At Hand

Inside any troubled and distressed mind
Is a perplex and heavy burden to carry
But try to have faith in the Lord to find
That haven of a peaceful pathway to tarry

From the warmth of your snug comfort zone
When your dreams have shattered in tatters
Just speak to the Lord to help soften the tone
For the very things in life that really matter

A few gentle words spoken within a sincere action
The unexplained feeling that someone truly cares
In a quietude of tranquillity when a soul is in reaction
Needed to heal desolation that the sad heart bares

The mind and body can capture its equilibrium tilt
Quelling the thirst of the spirit in a placid idle found
Deep heart-searching helps soothe the ravages in-built
And walking a new faith in a channel of solid ground

Octavia Hornby

30th July

On Being Assertive

A ssertive behaviour builds poise without pose
S elf-confidence from its maturity grows
S tand up for your rights, but respect other's views
E xamine your motives when options you choose
R espond positively to each situation
T hough negative thoughts form part of the equation
I nvest your time wisely, and good will ensue
V ery soon all will notice a happier you
E ach day will dawn bright when your attitude's right
N o adverse reactions, your outlook to blight
E xchange that transgression for prudent discretion
S hunning every expression of unjust aggression
S tems the tide that can override life's smooth progression

Ron Beaumont

30th July

Tree Of Life

Lean on me
let me bear your weight
I will be as a tree for you
I will be that strong for you
not as a mighty oak
standing tall
but as a willow
I will take the strain
my boughs will bend for you with you
and I will weep with you for you
lessening the pain
let my leaves gently billow in the wind
rustle in the rain
allow my branches to protect you
hung about you
wrapped around you like a veil
to shield you from the world
my trunk may not be thick nor long
but neither shall it crack break or fall
so lean on me be weaned by me
for my sap is sweet
and you can rest before me
then once refreshed walk away replete.

Fiona Jo Clark

Solitude

When I sit alone by myself
And gaze at the boundless sky,
Often I see a solitary bird,
Gliding gracefully above and so high,
Then I do not think myself, alone.
When I tread on ground or grass
Plants and trees and flowers I pass,
Flies buzz around and butterflies flutter,
Ants walk in line as if to class,
Then I do not think myself alone.
When I look at the pedestrian's path,
Cars and buses I see, on the road,
Tyres screech and horns honk out loud,
Faces glare from the advertisement board,
Then I do not think myself, alone.
As a busy day's work is at its end,
How time passed, how did it fly?
As stars appear and shine in the sky
Then I do not think myself, alone.
The day's work done and prayers said
With peace in my heart, no fears, no dread,
Then thoughts of a friend come to me,
A source of comfort and company,
Then I do not think myself, alone.
With faith in God, my Guardian Dear,
When He is near, I do not fear,
When a friend is sincere
And I have the courage to bear -
Then, I do not think myself alone.

Anjum Wasim Dar

31st July

Dragonflies Graze In The Wind

Light,
it flows and plunges deep,
far into the cauldron of our sky.
The dazzling blue echoing life,
is now encased in lurid grey.
But still the light sharpens its lance.

It is done.
The ground's brittle surface splits and fragments,
the haze of dust spirals, intertwines with the darkening sky.
The black mass erupts.
Sparks gash the brooding weight.
From the wounds, the deluge gushes out,
quenching the thirsty land.

I sit
in lush, vibrant, green grass,
sunlight flooding down,
highlighting dragonflies that graze in the wind,
while blackbirds indulge themselves
on branches dripping with plums.

I sit,
observe and think. Is it too late? I dream of hope.

Sigurd Ramans-Harborough

August

The day is bright and warm
Poppies mingle with the rustling corn
Harebells wave their purple bells
Honeysuckle streamers trail along the hedge
As thunder clouds form overhead

Woodland flowers reappear with faint perfume
Bluebells linger still
A late feast for the bees
Before the first sharp frost appears

Still the breeze is soft and warm
Water music escapes from unseen streams
The mighty oak and elm look on
To the bearded barley fields

A plentiful colourful display of butterflies
Picturesque against the many shades of green
And daises scattered round with open eye
As if drinking in the beauty of the scene before they fade and die

The warm air brings a rare perfume
Sweet birdsong rings
From the blackthorn bush
Delightful notes float through
The evening air
Over the sleeping earth a dreamy hush.

Beth Izatt Anderson

2nd August

One's Life

Life without you ambles along,
My heart is heavy, I know this is wrong.
There is so much to be thankful for,
Being miserable should be banned, against the law.
We all should be pleased as each new day dawns,
Fulfil it with happiness and be glad to be born.
We are so very lucky to be given a chance,
To make a difference, to sing, to dance,
To just do something, not to waste a day,
For life is for living, not to idle away.
When we lose someone dear we feel sad within,
Reality is a new phase must begin.
Helped my memories to face each day anew,
Some days will be harder for us to get through.
Look for the sunshine that radiates down,
Your loved one is present and all around.
Always remember your love never dies,
If you ever feel lonely look up to the skies.
The reassurance you need will always be there,
Yes you are loved and someone does care.

Anne Sackey

Peaceful Reflections

The fragrance of roses on the evening breeze
The quiet humming of the honeybees
What more on Earth is there so dear?
The bliss of Heaven ever near
As I walk in God's creation
My heart fills with pure elation
Such beautiful colours invade my eyes
In the garden that around me lies
The sweet smell of lavender fills the air
As I rest awhile without a care
For so rich is the scene a pure delight
On a soft and fragrant summer's night

Joan Constantine

3rd August

The Journey

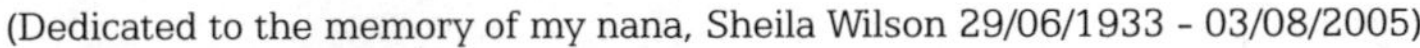

(Dedicated to the memory of my nana, Sheila Wilson 29/06/1933 - 03/08/2005)

As one falls cold
Then the journey starts to unfold
For the people who sleep do not rest
They fly like a free dove across a golden sky
Even a rocket couldn't go so high
They leave their loved ones behind
The ones that had lost their refine.

Yet this journey is ever so long
Until the hearing of the angels' song
Their voices enchanting your soul
There's a new chance today
A million stars coming your way
Their glow taking away sins and troubles before you reach home
It's when you realise you were never alone.

When the end of the journey is reached
The place where only happiness awaits
It's Heaven and you just know
A plain so beautiful no one can imagine
The journey needs no fear
For everyone will eventually end up here.

Kimberley Otter

Faith In The Lord

When our faith seems so small
Just look up to our Lord above
For He really does care for us all
Through His bountiful love

God protects us, when troubles are nigh
Maybe, upon a cold windy day
When the wind is blowing so boisterously high
With faith, just look up and pray

The winds will cease, incredibly
And there will be calm once again
For the Lord will answer, you may see
Such faith you will regain

When the weather is unbearably hot
Throughout the summertime
And lightning strikes, like a shot
And thunder roars in rhyme

Do not be afraid, even then
For God will be quite near
If we turn to the Lord, where and when
We have faith, our good God will surely hear

Jean P McGovern

The Mendip Hills

To see the beauty of the Mendip Hills
When night approaches the air roars at will
The sun upon a summer evening is high in the sky
Then I saw a lone hawk hovering before my eyes

I come on holidays to Somerset and stay each year
When the country air smells fresh when the sky is clear
Thro' the summer the hot sun tans my pale face
The sheer beauty of a cider orchard is added to its grace

Those once green fields have become a beautiful shade of golden brown
The ferns upon the hill changes colour when the sun beams down
To travel thro' those bending narrow country lanes
When you pass a small grey stone church with a weathervane

There are scenes thro' the years that time stood still
Only Mother Nature can restore the beauty of the hills
When the old trees died their offspring fills the place
The ripening hay is cut, the young grass is soft like lace

So enjoy the beauty of the Mendip green covered hills
When the countryside awakes when the hawks looks for its kill
Then admire the beauty, it's Somerset's wonderful pleasure
When you stroll thro' the countryside you see its treasures

J F Grainger

Recipe To Happiness

Take a cup of kindness
Fill it up with love
Add a touch of essence
From the sun above
A spoon of sweetness from the heart
A salty tear or two
Mix them all with joy and laughter
Now all you have to do
Is to make a wish for others
For all their dreams to come true
Then you will find a happiness
To last your whole life through.

Dorothy Ledger

6th August

Another Day

When it all began, I was sitting in the garden,
My mobile beside me, and I remembered.
The memories flowed and floated like the puffy white clouds above me,
Today is the anniversary of my daughter's wedding,
When I danced all evening with all the men,
I was the mother-of-the-bride,
A privileged place, a happy time.

Forty years on and we're celebrating again,
I'm now a grandmother and a great-grandmother;
A privileged place, a happy time.

What fun we'll have today,
As I hold another new baby in my arms,
Whilst others dance.
A privileged place, a happy time.

The phone rings, 'I'm ready,' I say, 'pick me up.'

Sylvia Scoville

7th August

Above Ripponden

In the blue of the night, spiders weave
Their intricate awning.
Anchored 'twixt grasses they glistening leave
The dew of the dawning.

Ginger grass runs over hills in a swathe,
Flamboyantly flowing.
A deep undulating Mexican wave,
Rippling, ever widening.

Skylark, hovering in high song flight,
He's warbling and trilling.
Notes melting into the perfect light,
He pipes on untiring.

Look. See on the hills the round sun fling
A golden adorning.
In thanks for these gifts I have to sing
On this summer morning.

Heather Ferrier

8th August

The Sprees Of The Ocean Seas

All the seasides and global waters provide
The exact laughs and kiteful rights for the gemstone children
Who tell funny jokes to each other while watching
The mermaids doing their butterfly dances
Next to the dolphins who both know the exact patterns
To take when going over the tidal waves
As they can see all the affections and reflections
From the starfish inside the ocean's bubbles
That never do deals within any troubles
Even all the seaweeds have their good points
And deeds for all the octopuses who love their nature's finest feels
While making seaweed necklaces for all the Moby Dicks
Who can then provide extra tricks for their sweethearts
Who know all the tastes from the ocean's fruits
Which know all the harvests from inside the rapids
And currents that can feel
All the inside outs of the whirlpools
Upon the seas kingdoms and graces.

Steven Pearson

Life

Pompously they sit, their lips held tight,
Whilst silently we reflect, our thoughts, in the black of night.
The closeness of individuals and those who really care,
Against the sadness of those who generate spiteful despair.
Control of your life, seems to lie with another,
To which you ask, 'Oh just don't bother!'
You can't do your best, you're scared by their might.
You can have a view, but it cannot be right.
The darkness in your mind, damning you by its power.
The cold black bricks of an extending tower.
'Why?' is your question, 'Can you take any more?'
Your best is not good enough; your best is just poor!

But the answers lie in your faith, soul and vigour,
If you know your worth, then others do not figure.
Help yourself, make your soul become strong,
Help yourself, you've done no wrong.

Like them, help them, until you win,
Seek peace in them, forgive their sin.
Be strong, be bold, be proud and smile,
The importance is life, and that is worthwhile.

Colin Wallace

10th August

Ode To Summer

The sweet scent of flowers in the air
The song of the birds at morn
The beauty of a full-blown rose
Drinking the dew at dawn

White clouds scudding by in an azure blue sky
Like lambs in a frolicking dance
The hills in their patchwork quilt of green
Such scenes cannot fail to entrance

Hedgerows and trees fully clothed once again
Yellow primroses once more on view
The warmth of the sun at the height of the day
And the sea in its cool dress of blue

These are the beauties that nature controls
In her own inimitable way
So that summer awakes refreshed and serene
Its new magic each year to display

Maureen Quirey

11th August

Kingfisher Morning

Imagine a morning with sky bright and blue
All cotton wool clouds and grass wet with dew
Imagine a morning with birdsong so sweet
All daisies and buttercups arrayed round your feet
Imagine a morning by cool rippling stream
As low on a tree branch a flash of blue's seen
Imagine a morning all shining and new
So lovely the dawning, all kingfisher blue.

Joan Winwood

12th August

Footprints

There is nothing in life that is already written
No predefinition of how we live or who we love.
Each life is just a walk along a broad avenue of sand
Time, the ebb and flow of an unfathomable ocean

Each moment just a footprint,
Washed away.

Our footprints linger in the danger of deep water
Lie invisible in the safety of dry land

We should not look back on footprints lost
Or peer forward to see where they might lead
We should not look down to covet every impression
Stand still to feel the sand between our toes

Or be fooled into believing
We walk alone.

Pat Geeson

Beyond The Storm

There was no escaping the tempest's rage,
The oppressive clouds, the rainstorm's rampage;
It had to be faced, there was nowhere to hide,
- Too far to the shelter to creep inside;
The temperature dropped, all senses were numb,
I braced myself for the moment had come;
'No pity, no pity', the thunder roared
While the lightning waved high its twin-forked sword;
The downpour that once was far out at sea,
Now swept up the shoreline, engulfing me;
There seemed no end to this cold, wet, dark world
Where the black clouds above just swirled and swirled;
Then a peephole to Heav'n showed in the sky,
A break in the furore the wind drove by -
An oasis of peace, stillness so blue,
A gap in the tempest where God broke through
And called out to me the future to view.

David Radford

13th August

A Summer Sunday

A summer Sunday by the Dee,
Its calming waters drifting by,
Can set all troubled spirits free
Beneath a blue and tranquil sky.

Old Chester city's Roman wall
Is backdrop to the Sunday scene;
That conjures history to enthral
Of ancient people who have been.

Lazily drooping willow trees
With wispy branches silver green,
Enhance an atmosphere of ease
As by the water's edge they lean.

The snow-white swans all radiant,
Gracefully preening as they glide,
Are so serene and elegant
Whilst padding feet below they hide.

While rowers pulling on their oars
Propel the river boats along,
The watching people on the shores
Just sit relaxing in the sun.

Cautious children, with such delight,
Feed ducks and pigeons close to hand;
Until the birds take sudden flight
When play is struck up by the band.

All kinds of folk just ambling by
From simple pleasure they derive;
For cares and woes to pacify
And feeling good to be alive.

Bill Newham

13th August

Tomorrow's Nebulae

Yesterday
An empty void,
A vacuum of infinite space.
Conceptual wilderness,
Where baron stars cry in lonely nebulae.

Today
An expanse of vibrant colour,
Shatteringly bright festive happiness.
Intangible perfection,
Where any concept is possibly perfect.

Tomorrow
An entity of hope,
A future of noble belief.
Indefinable glory,
Where creation is bliss and tranquil commune exists.

Sean I Riley

14th August

The Sun Is Making Grapes Today

The sun is making grapes today,
The clouds are pillows in the sky,
Green grass is singing to the stones,
The wind kisses each butterfly.

It takes a long, long summertime
To see the beauty everywhere,
And sometimes in a quiet place
Thank God with a little prayer.

Marion Schoeberlein

15th August

A Great Blue Sky

It is early summer, our England nestles under a great blue sky,
A few billowing clouds meander gently by.
A pleasant breeze is wafting off the sea,
The sun beams down making it a wonderful day for you and me.

Our countryside is lush and green,
Everywhere thrusting nature is to be seen.
Our feathered friends busily feed their hungry brood,
The chicks always impatient to get their food.

The fallow deer, the lowing cattle chew the vibrant pasture,
They feed in total comfort and leisure.
The vixen is guarding her cubs around her den,
The fox is hunting, hoping to catch a big juicy hen.

The colourful kingfisher is perching beside the riverbank waiting
For the fish to rise, its future ended, there is no debating.
The farmer's fields, ploughed, sowed, now filled with their designated crop
To many it would be a disaster if we didn't produce a pleasure giving hop.

With good winter rains the rivers, streams and reservoirs are filled to the brim,
Enabling our fish stocks to thrive and swim.
We rest, play, picnic, love, in the shade of a great oak tree
We relax and let our thoughts and dreams roam free.

Mother Nature in her benevolence makes it a great world in which to stay,
That it will continue we sincerely hope and pray.
To our Eternal Father who sits on his throne most high,
It would be wonderful if we could sit for ever under a great blue sky.

Terry Godwin

16th August

Word Without End

Books are full of wisdom
and words as wise as sage
yet archived dry and dusty
are the words of bygone age.

The warring words of ancient worlds
slumber undisturbed
covers cracked from side to side
but pages unperturbed.

Dynasties have raised their flag
and fallen in the field
kings and queens have come and gone
their reigns are unrevealed.

Jenny spins industrial
Stephenson has steam
achievements that are laid to rest
where light shall never gleam.

Yet pull this one book from the shelf
and treat it as a friend
a travelling companion true
until this age shall end.

This book has healed the leper
this book has raised the dead
this book has brought the blind their sight
this book has bruised and bled.

This book it does not threaten
it does not seize by force
it leads you gently to the Lord
when life has run its course.

Sean Kinsella

17th August

The Moors In Summer

One day the moor forgot,
Traditional dark and gloom,
Flirted free with summer,
Bright with golden gorse and broom.

Little birds like arrows,
Flew from the quiet heather,
The sky was calm and blue,
As warm as wine the weather.

The cotton grass grew by pools,
Like fallen stars reflected,
From galaxies above,
On Earth now resurrected.

As if some magic wand,
Had touched path and hill and crag,
With new spellbinding beauty,
Under the elfin flag.

Another face of moorland,
By field and wood and farm,
Mysterious and strange,
That had the power to charm.

Kathleen Scatchard

17th August

How Did I Live Without Him?

How did I live without Him?
Not to know His wonderful Son
Who came to Earth to save us
And after His work was done
He rose and went to Heaven
To wait for us to come.

How did I cope without Him?
How did I manage at all?
My life confused and muddled
On the edge where I would fall
Into pits of great depression
There was no one there to call.

Now I've found my Saviour
My life is clear to see
All problems, they are sorted
And God to comfort me
Never more to be alone
I give myself to Thee.

C M Armstrong

18th August

Swizzle Sticks And Cocktails

Under an azure sky kamikaze wasps dived,
Became a hazard as I stirred my swizzle stick
Slowly around and round the cocktail by my side.
The zephyr of a warm summer's evening caressed,
It carried the scent of roses and salt sea air,
And as the sun sank to the horizon and paused,
I thought of a far distant kibbutz and bazaar,
With orchards of oranges and people dancing.
The jacuzzi like a cannibals cooking pot
Was bubbling away down in deepest Africa,
Where the tzetze fly bite, staring vultures give fright,
And zebra move in a blurred haze of shimmering heat,
While natives played tunes on kazoos, antelopes grazed.
The cold terrazzo patterned floor beneath my feet
Reminded me of Rome, jezebels mesmerised
And bartered, the piazza provided food and wine.
The ice sculptor carried thoughts of White Russia
And the cruel dictatorial Tsars in times now past,
White blinding blizzards, wizened wizards casting spells,
As they puzzled turning lead into gold at last.
The evening quiz game had started without me,
Was full of zany puzzling bizarre questions.
Looked to the zenith, thousands of stars I could see,
The Milky Way a dazzling necklace of diamonds.
Bronzed Amazonian nubile nymphs hand in hand
Passed with their Adonises, gentle music drifts.
Ocean liners anchored offshore ablaze with light,
Sat like tethered dogs longing for the open sea.
A brazier nearby glowed as I gently dozed,
The cocktails made my vision fuzzy, my eyes glazed,
I guzzled the last drops then head for my bed
With a muzzy head from swizzle sticks and cocktails.

David M Walford

18th August

Thunder

Mist moves across fields
and flowers shiver, while
petals turn inwards,
reaching back to buds hiding
from thunder that shakes
buildings around this place.
I feel torn apart but then
the sun shines, new strength
comes from strange sources:
seeds take root, trees grow
to great heights, making me
wonder how I ever doubted
this force, this everlasting force
that moves me on and on.

Mary Guckian

19th August

Barbecue Season

The barbecue season arrives once more, much to my chagrin,
When everyone sees himself as a trendy sort of bloke
Tries to light his damp charcoal to sacrifice some meat:
Then some soppy bleeder chucks on a gallon of paraffin,
And soon the air is filled with thick black choking acrid smoke,
Then chicken Hiroshima is the Sunday tea time treat.

There's Nagasaki sausages and Belsen burgers too,
And fresh cremated corn upon the cob,
So B&Q and Alka-Seltzer rub their hands with glee:
It's chewier and tougher than the sole upon your shoe,
You're dicing with a painful death if it goes near your gob,
At best it's salmonella, or p'raps even CJD.

Mick Nash

Wedding Wishes

Fancy dresses, suit and tie,
Love and kisses that make you cry,
Confetti, toasts and wedding cake,
With gifts, friends, flowers and vows to make,

But ...
When today's a treasured memory,
You both cherish and hold dear,
When tomorrow's an adventure,
To be faced without a fear,
There's only one thing matters,
Amidst all the tears and laughter,
It's the *love* you both believe in,
And the *happy ever after*.

Susan Geldard

Before My Eyes

I looked into the picture
of the deep blue sky,
trapped within my window frame.
On and on I searched hopelessly,
for a glint from the starless sky.
My eyes fell down in disappointment.
A street lamp caught my attention
then I understood, oh God.
A sea of lights before my eyes,
and I did not realise.

Adeola Oluwadamilola Adekoya

20th August

A Time Of Beauty

The abundancy of fruit on the trees
From apples to acorns and ripe cherries
Roses, pansies and a host of flowers
Will keep the bumblebees busy for hours
Over meadows lush, butterflies dance
Below them wildlife prance
Rabbits burrowing, birds gliding through the air
Foxes, venturing from their lair
Deer are darting to and fro
Squirrels about their business go
Sunshine bright and clear blue skies
Brightly coloured dragonflies
A time of beauty to linger on
All too soon summer will be gone

Gertrude Schöen

21st August

Mirages

Now morning with
Its shaft of light
Chases the stars
Back to the night.

Then dawns pink
Fingertip is born
To herald the sun
As it greets the morn.

And as it rises
In the sky
Searching out the shadows
Chasing the night away

We watch! And stand upon
The threshold of the day
And ponder on our dreams
That we have lost along the way.

But the thoughtful
Soul dreams on
In solitude, remembers
Things that were undone.

And we who realize today
That those desires
We lost along the way
They were just mirages!

Like water in the sand
And mirages like dreams
They fade away
As if erased by some gigantic hand.

But we whose spirit is unbowed
Will dream a better dream today.

Joan May Wills

Storms Of Life

When the waves lift me high
In the storms of life
My Saviour comes to me
With His words of comfort I ride the crests
Until the land I see
In the murky darkness of the night
I cry out unto Him
His word comes as a light for my path
Then my spirit rests in Him.

Patricia Raisôn

Great Creator

Grant us this day holistic healing
Of body - mind - and spirit.

Grant us not a different day from others,
But sufficiently good health and strength,
Energy and resources to meet each need
As we come to it.

May our love for *You* be in loving others ...
Our service to You be in serving others ...
Our hearing You in hearing others ...

May *peace* this day be in You
May *peace* this day be with You
May *peace* this day come from You.

Clive Cornwall

23rd August

Encountering A Dolphin

Often he leaps skyward,
soaring for the heavens,
trusting the water to catch him.

His ascent is acrobatic,
playfully defying logic,
screeching in mid-air.

His landing uncluttered.
Aquatic, silent, clean.
Barely a ripple disturbed.

His smile remains constant,
enchanting, disarming,
transparent like a child's.

His chuckle infectious,
splintering detachment.
Melting, the hardest of hearts.

Paul Kelly

Open my eyes, O Lord
To your mysteries divine
Let my understanding
Be just as clear as thine
Let me turn to You in love
And know that You are watching
From way up above
My trust has never faded
All my life I trust in You
Give me tolerance to sustain me
And love will shine through.

Mary Tickle

24th August

Flowers

Flowers,
Alive
For but
A day
Or
Perhaps
A longer
Stay?

Nicola Barnes

Horizons

A distant journey, a far-off place,
escaping the rat race,
working all week for a weekend away.
Just throw caution to the wind,
got to get away at the break of day.
A time to love, a time to laugh.
Tap your feet, cruise up and down the main street,
as for the in-crowd, it's where we meet.
A twilight world away from the working day.

Jonathan Covington

25th August

Count My Blessings

(Dad, you are forever in my thoughts!)

I live, but I have lost
My partner, my friend, my soulmate.
I live, but I have lost
The life we shared together.
I live, but I have lost
The couples we had as friends.

I live, but count my blessings
For my lovely home and my wheels.
I live, but count my blessings
For my health and my lifestyle.
I live, but count my blessings
For my family and friends.

I live and must be strong
For my children and grandchildren.
I live and must be stronger
For my friends and my neighbours.
I live and must be even strong
Left with my memories ... as life goes on!

Janet L Stephenson

Summer Glory

Path of chamomile, white daisies on emerald green,
A soft carpet fit for a queen.
Adjacent fields of golden corn, the sun has borne.
Wild honeysuckle in the hedgerow adds sweet fragrance to the air.
The sun breaks through a sky of blue.
Tiny birds shuffle in the dusty soil as though wishing it was still a pool.
In the distance a combine works away, soon harvest time will be over
And the chamomile path will lose its glory for another year.

Jean Bailey

26th August

Watching the clouds roll slowly by,
shapes and faces high in the sky.
White and fluffy, oyster and grey,
as Earth meets sky - no rush today.

My eyes look up to the heavens above,
completely enveloped in the Saviour's love.
The sun is low and hidden from view,
shafts of light like a beacon shine through.

A lake of mist rising gently around,
ribbons of moisture circle the ground.

Looking out on this ghostly array,
a lone walker with his dog at play -
before my eyes - it seems unreal.

I capture the moment forever to seal;
the presence of God is here to feel.

Jean Jackson

27th August

The Summer Sun

I walked in the park,
Watched the birds flit from tree to tree,
Their flitting a sign of joy.

I looked up to the sun in the sky
And saw the yellow and gold orb
Spread wide and clear in the midst of the blue sky,
Saw the rays it projected,
Like tentacles of glory light
Released in the midst of darkness to
Wash away the burdens of hurt and blinded spirit.

I saw the new light of white, blue, black,
Red and purple amidst a spangling of gold
Released like smiling kisses of hellos and welcomes
On brows furrowed with worldly concerns.

I saw flowers, daffodils, daisies and buttercups
Each one clothed with such shimmering light,
With the honeybees buzzing happily and noisily around.

I saw a garden of awesome beauty with trees
Like armoured soldiers and leaves that
Swayed in the noonday breeze.

I saw all these and knew that it was well.

Annoha Kyeremeh

28th August

Gliding Along

On a warm June evening
Boarding the Victoria Barge
Remembering! Here at Paper Mill Lock
Gone the horse drawn barges
48 men! Women! Maddie a polio victim carried on board.

The boat invaded! The calm water
Gently creating ripples
Among giant buttercup lilies
Blue swordfish flies! Caress the water
A guard of honour! Green reeds stand tall
Complimenting our eyes
Forget-me-nots, wild plants, age long trees
Ducks sheltering under foliage.

Approaching 600 year old Oulton Church
We see campers having super
Reversing! Homeward bound
Dining! Prawns, paté, cheese, strawberries, cakes
How peaceful! to glide along
Red sunset! Mooring!
Having enjoyed nature's grandeur.

Patricia Turpin

Summer Twilight

Still,
How still,
No movement,
Smells compete,
Souls to drown, tranquillity feat.
No whisper clouds,
Paint the sky,
No passing breeze,
Float butterflies.

Still,
So still,
Summer twilight,
Denim blue,
Shading down,
Hue by hue,
Crescent moon,
Twilight gem,
Hung in splendour,
Lord's diadem.

Calm,
So calm,
The summer day,
Winding down,
Laying aside,
Heaven's gown,
Lord's gift,
View of share,
Whose magnificence
Fills my prayer.

Alvin Creighton

30th August

Carpe Diem

Why is life?
What purpose does life hold
For people so bold?
Some people would gladly spend an eternity
Searching for the key
To an unsolvable riddle,
But not me.

Truth is, no one will ever know
Why we are here on show.
So why then should we spend
Our lives till the end
In pursuit of a solution
To an unanswerable question?

Why must we spend our days
Questioning our ways?
This to me is a waste,
We are around for such short space,
That to question it, is to be illogical.
In my opinion we should live life to its full,
We should live every day like it's our last,
Not living for what's happened back in the past.

Carpe diem ...

It's Latin. 'Seize the day'.
It means to live life and pray
That you awake the following day
To live it again in a different way.

This friends, is the meaning of life.
Be happy, don't worry and ignore the strife,
Live for you, for others will follow,
Mould your own life; it's your own dough,
Don't be a sheep and bleat with the flock,
Be different, be the cream of the crop.

This is life.
Live it.

Liam Bagnall

At The End Of The Day

(Written in loving memory of my beloved grandmother, Lavina Pask)

As I sit in the peace at the end of the day,
The sun setting slow in the sky,
Reflecting a while on all that has been,
Time ticking the evening by.

Each day, as it dawns, can bring many things,
With the crispness of morning dew,
The beauty the Earth has given to us,
We view it for free, me and you.

The people we meet along life's path,
Say hello and give them a smile,
Help someone out, make someone laugh,
Rest now and chat for a while.

Take time for a friend, call just to say,
How are you? To show that you care,
Letting the ones who you love, so dear,
Know that you'll always be there.

Spend all your days with hope in your heart,
With a sprinkling of peace and love.
Be thankful for all of the blessings you have,
Given by the good Lord above.

The kindness that you would wish for yourself,
Show it in all that you say,
So, as I sit in the peace at the end of the day,
I'm contented that I lived my life in this way.

K E Harrod

September Again

September again, we reflect and remember,
The months have flown by, we are nearer December,
Hedgerows are tired, the harvest is in,
Swallows in clusters, their time to take wing,
Sunflowers nod, face the shortening day,
Farmers so busy, with the last of the hay,
Leaves turning brown, start fluttering down,
The pavements soon covered in a slippery gown,
September again, our summer's slipped by,
Swallows now leaving for South African skies.

Winifred Curran

Seeds Of Faith

Make me a sower of your seeds,
bring forth the blooms
and blossoms of your love,
May your fragrance linger
when you pass by.
The grace of Heaven
touching those you love.

Make me a sower of your seeds,
may my lips speak the
gospel of your love.
Bring hope to those
in doubt,
light of faith to
those without.

Make me a sower of your seeds,
my ways to follow
the Lord's good deeds.
With heart and soul
willing to pray;
inclined to listen
to what God has to say.

Make me a sower of your seeds,
the harvest to be
gathered by God's hand;
Man the willing worker
in the vineyard.
By seeds of faith,
Lord help us to understand.

Robert Waggitt

3rd September

Shadows In The Firelight

As evening draws to eventual close,
Thoughts turn to reflect and interpose.
How as my coal fire steadily ebbs
Into dying cinders, the walls turn and twist in mystifying webs.
I see a chariot racing across the ceiling,
A spider's nest, and cobwebs revealing
The chances I've missed, in life - concealing
But hopes forever boosting my feeling
My eyes drift thoughtless, trying to find a meaning
Surely I've given something to life?
Not just a hollow, senseless stealing
Of moments when I've carried all before me,
When God persevered with a soul, not worth a fee.
So there, you see - my many mongrels I've acquired.
I see them all before me, on the walls,
Flickering, barking, all retired, like me.
Although the shadows begin to fade
And darkness descends to quiet solitude,
I still attempt to resurrect happy days we spent
Just watching the mist, gathering at dawn,
Or rainbows threatening to spoil the morn,
A chaffinch throbbing, like acres of corn,
Bobbing and weaving like threads of gold - reborn
Shadows - don't leave me - upon the wall.

A Boddison

4th September

Untitled

When tiredness creeps o'er you
And you've had a busy day,
Before you sigh - and close your eye
Just pause a while, and say ...

Have I worked hard enough today
And given of my best,
Have I loved enough today
And shared it with the rest.

Have I shared another's load
And helped him on his way
Have I heard my neighbour
When he cried for help today.

Well Lord, I've tried, and if I failed,
I ask but this of Thee,
I'll try harder still tomorrow,
But tonight, watch over me.

John Gowans

School Days

Nursery days are over now,
You are five next year.
Growing up, going into reception class,
Brings a few nervous but happy tears.

Always remember your childhood,
Happy days at school too,
Because these years go by so fast,
Soon they are over and through.

A happy part of your life.
I hope we can watch as you grow
And turn from a lovely girl, our daughter,
Into a woman, a mother and a wife.

Trudie Sullivan

5th September

Stepping Stones

Crossing over a river, with the greatest of all care,
Using old stepping stones, someone had placed there.
The river swirled around wildly, so dark, deep and grey,
A thought flashed right by me, as if an angel did relay.
The stepping stones are alike our own goodness within,
Where we've yet done right, caused no harm, evil or sin.
A safe place, yes, a haven, to oft run to time and again,
Somewhere of much safety, without any fear or pain,
Yet the water swirling about is life's own darkest fears,
The bad points, the depths, hidden anguish that often rears.
It waits here forever, for just one slip to pull us down,
It's every tear, all our pain, our every worry or frown.
By looking ahead clearly, stepping over each stone,
Concentrating carefully, you'll find your way home.
Just as we reach the other side, often safe and secure,
There's angels waiting at death's door to assure.
Yet, let's say we slip and fail to pull ourselves out,
Darkness awaits us, endless terrors without a doubt.
Why worry about stepping stones, or should you slip,
If you've no worry for life, the times you fall or trip?
Life is those stepping stones and all that we ever do,
The depth of deep water ever swirls around us it's true.
This was an inspired blessing yet a call to one and all.
Tread life's stepping stones cautiously, it's so easy to fall.

C R Slater

Thought Of The Day

Prayer is the opening of the heart to God as to a friend,
Step to Jesus pocket prayer, does not change God, but

It does change us, and our relation to God, it places us in the
Channel of blessing, and in that frame of mind in which God

Can consistently and safely grant our request, how shall
We pray so as to be heard and to receive help? For one thing,

There must be a real desire in our hearts, forms of words do
Not make prayer, we must want something and must realise

Our dependence upon God for it, prayer is the key in the hand
Of faith to unlock Heaven's storehouse, where are treasured
The boundless of omnipotence.

Imogene Lindo

What About You?

Music enchants the broken
heart. It sends the blues
away. What about you?
Art stops the worries.
Literature melts your opinions,
in time for change to arrive.
What about you?
Does the question make
love a problem?

Kirk Antony Watson

8th September

Prayer For The World

World
I remembered you in my prayers last night
Not on my knees with my eyes shut tight
But standing at the window
Gazing at God's handiwork, the evening star;
And I asked Him to bless you
All you needy ones
You who are sick and dying
You who are bound in poverty
You who are homeless
You who cry out for justice
You who desire peace
All you, His children
Wherever you are.

M Spence

If ever you need a friend,
then I'll be there for you.

If ever you need a shoulder to cry on,
then I'll be there for you.

If ever you feel lonely, sad or blue,
Remember ... I will always be there for you.

Sara Crump

10th September

Jesus

He is the Creator, the Beginning and End,
the Alpha and Omega, yet calls me His friend.
The Word and the Witness, also the True Vine
some know Him as Jesus, the Saviour Divine.
The Rose of Sharon, the Shepherd, we're sheep
The life, the Resurrection, now no need to weep.
He's the Lion, the Lily and yes, He's the Lamb
And the scriptures remind me, He is the I Am
He's the only begotten, the Father's dear Son,
the Saviour of sinners and blest Holy One.
Immanuel God with us it's said He would be,
He's God's Beloved Son who died on a tree
The King of all Ages, as well as the Jews
and He is Messiah, the Christ, the Good News.
The Author of Life, the conqueror of Hell,
The Lord of Glory, where believers shall dwell.
The Horn of Salvation, new life He brings
Apostle, high priest, He taught us great things.
Wonderful Counsellor, Mighty God is He.
I know Him as Jesus and Jesus love me.

Albert Watson

A Peaceful World

Live peacefully with all men,
'Behold I make all things new'.
Bless those who persecute even when destitute
These are the things God has told us to do.
Rejoice with those who do rejoice
Weep with those who weep,
By obeying His commandments
The world could find such peaceful sleep.
Recompense to no man evil for evil,
'Vengeance is mine, I will repay!'
Care for creation, find joy in rebuilding
The words of God's wisdom are needed today.
Rejoice in all hope and in all tribulation
Praise Him in prayer, thank Him for a life
Feel His forgiveness for every temptation,
His gracious mercies can banish all strife.
Renewal of mind can prove what is good,
Loving and giving to live as we should.
Feed those who are hungry, let them see
The power of the spirit within us, hour after hour.
Owe no man anything, love one another
Neighbours and enemies love as a brother.
With holiness, graciousness, banners unfurled
All striving to live in a new peaceful world.

Elsie G B Horrocks

11th September

Jesus My Lord

You came from Heaven,
My glorious King,
On Calvary's tree, there
You pardon my sin
Oh glory hallelujah
Praise Your wonderful name
For I've found life eternal
On Your heavenly plain.

Jesus my Lord
Thy love is precious to me.
My desire is always to be near You
Jesus my Lord.

Come into my heart Lord
Don't leave me alone
For life without You
I will not condone
You came from glory
To free me from sin
And You loved me so dearly
To my heart enter in.

Barbara Jean Whelan

A Prayer Poem

Disperse my worries, O Lord
until silence speaks
through Your calm, gentle voice.
Turn me from the pain of anxiety
and thoughts that tangle the mind,
the confusion of the maze of life,
to waiting,
listening,
praying,
trusting,
peace.

Wendy Dedicott

12th September

Reflections Of Inner Peace

A confidence that shines through to reflect inner-confidence
Portrays a belief in myself which comes from the heart
As each obstacle is overcome with tenacity and endurance
I face tomorrow filled with vigour and enthusiasm.

Freedom expresses deep feelings which were once kept inside
Bursting into a wonderful expression of happiness untold
Reflections of life and love presented in music and poetry
Are the way forward into a world where talents are now recognised.

As I continue to express just what I feel in my heart
My whole life has turned into a beautiful multitude of feelings
Making the past just a memory to learn from and treasure
Strength within expresses a true reflection
Of inner peace and contentment.

Marjory Price

Alone

Alone on a hilltop I stand,
My mind wandering, as I watched,
Looking for comfort and assurance,
For in actual fact, I am never quite alone.

The dawn lined with white fleecy clouds,
Like a cotton field ready for picking.
Birds chirping and singing love songs,
The feeling of spring is in the air.

Now the time has come,
To put the past behind,
Preparations must be made,
For life is for today and tomorrow.

As the morning mist lifts it passes me by,
Sending shivers down my spine,
Whispering gently in my ear,
You are not alone.

Reach out, for God is always there,
His footprints in the sand,
His signature painted on all things beautiful.
Reach out, for God is always there.

Trees whisper in the wind,
Memories have flown,
Good memories will be back,
And friends we shall always have.

Reach out,
Give a friend a call,
Write a letter or email,
For today I shall never be alone again.

Nadine Mackie

13th September

The World Through The Window

When down at heart, what lifts your spirits?
I stand by the window and gaze
The world of my overgrown garden
Can brighten the darkest of days

An old plastic tub full of water
Plus pondweed, a stone and a log
- An eyesore for certain, but precious -
Is home to a large, handsome frog

And each time I glance through the window
I check for a weed-covered bump
For frog loves to hang in the water
Or sit on the log, primed to jump

And as for the birds - what a blessing!
They cheer me, whatever my mood
My dear, hungry friends - how rewarding
To watch them come down for their food

Doves, starlings, tits, dunnocks - one robin
The sparrows, so cheeky and smart
And blackbird, so focused and busy
Two bullfinches, never apart

And let's not forget Outlaw Squirrel
Who moves with such beauty and grace
Those neat little hands - how exquisite
And what an adorable face!

So if you feel down, look around you
Or listen, quite still, for a while
There's sure to be something that pleases
That comforts or forces a smile.

Helen M Clarke

A Day Is Born

The bird's sweet song
Disturbs the hush of morn
Another night has flown
A day is born
How sweet to know
He waits
And at the break
Of each new day
His loving hand
Holds out the way

Jennifer René Daniel

15th September

The Light

Glossed with fruit, and gleaming with shining rays,
Creating head pains through this gaze.
Eyes meet, and my heart is prepared,
Pounding vastly my blood is, pumping my veins.
As though it was an international ranged train,
Decreasing weight below certain standard.

Vision only stares at a light figure,
No body as though it appears slowly.
Eyesight adjusts straight for faithful thoughts,
Troubled before, as I was wondering negatively.
Body appears, as I suddenly drop to my knees,
Startled at this memorable gaze.

Long hair and white robe as clear as spiritual vision,
Brown sandals as John used as an example.
Heavenly choir sing in the misty background,
Signalling the figure approaching closer
Paralysed physically without feelings of fear,
My knowledge blows to find it's *Jesus.*

Charlie Kwame Maguire (14)

15th September

A Thank You

I have this day awoken from my sleeping hours to
see once more the beauty - the wonders in our world,
from the very Earth - to the heights of Heaven's skies - there
are endless wonders to meet our eyes - birds of nature -
in full flight - clouds floating with total ease in vast open
skies - while on the Earth there are wonders growing at our
feet - every flower seen has a real beauty, all its very own.

What more could I request? I am alive and feeling well -
I have friends that share good things with me - I have
nature's wonders on Earth and in vast skies - may I
remember to keep a thank you - ready of my lips.

Rowland Patrick Scannell

Bright Light

Whatever secretes within the bright light
Stays hidden well,
Behind the plausible smile
The upbeat stance,
The impenetrable optimism;
What private hell,
What darkest mile,
What shadowed dance,
What black rainbow prism?

No one knows what haunts the bright light,
And no one can tell,
For lonely are the brave,
In their secret wars,
Their conflicts undefined;
What dreams compel,
What thoughts so grave,
What grim detours,
What rules their mind?

There is no discerning
What the bright light does not shine upon,
Nor refuses to show
Or illuminate of the loved and lost and gone
Like the flowers buried in the snow.

Tony Bush

Snippets

Random -
Scattered thoughts thrown
against walls crumbled down.

Spent; tireless worry creasing foreheads,
lines of misunderstanding,
lines of distrust,
of anger,
of horror,
of love.

Depleted energy supplies,
staggered mind drifts
like snow banks hiding the truth.

Predetermined, post-traumatic
endless snippets of memories
family encased surroundings -
shared laughter.

Yet ...

Worries, monetary substance
as roofs need work,
walls painted,
sheet rock fixed.

Home improvement hell
beginning with reddened eyes -

Self-pity surmounting
as goals for self-improvement
remain steadfast.

Random Sunday mornings
with too little sleep.

Melissa Halidy

17th September

Prayer For The Motorway

Designers, who in cool Japan
Bend metal into swaddling bands,
Creators of the cradle that we travel in tonight,
In you we trust.

Controllers of the robot arm
That welds and stamps each body part
To curvilinear grace,
Please keep us safe.
For in your hollow crumple zones
We place our children's green stick bones
And fire them down the barrel of the night.

As darkness licks the headlight's beam,
We wipe the breath that clouds the screen,
And pray that hand and eye and nerve
Will keep us on the sickle curve
That turns aside the terrors of the night.

But tight inside our oyster shell
Of toughened glass and tempered steel,
Despairing of the unmarked road tonight,
We turn to search inside ourselves,
And in the silent space find seeds of faith,
A hardening string of pearls
Between our fingers on the motorway tonight.

Anna Bacon

Untitled

(Addressed to a child)

You shouldn't become bitter
because then you would
act like them, them when they
make you bitter, let it go
for your own sake, for the
sake of your life, and breathe
breathe a sigh, a resignation
and keep your heart carefree.
Don't allow the worst of them
to make you bitter - breathe it
out, breathe ... they're wrong
but open your heart again if
you dare to, and let it, let it go.

P T Barron

18th September

Peace

What is a thing called peace?
The answer - when all war doth cease,
Tranquillity each hour, each day,
Troubles calmed in every way.

Peace each moment truly brings,
Joy to every living thing,
Peace of mind - peace from stress,
A lovely form of happiness.

Peace from worries, peace from pain,
What a blessing - so to gain,
If peace in life means anything,
Bless each hour that peace doth bring.

P M Peet

19th September

A Birthday Prayer

(Dedicated to my sister, Rosalie)

Soften my heart, Lord Jesus
Soften my heart each day.
Soften my heart, Lord Jesus
As I endeavour to walk in Your way.

Give me the strength, Lord Jesus
To help others in deep despair.
Give me the strength, Lord Jesus
As I endeavour to show them I care.

Take control of my vision, Lord Jesus
As I look to a world that is lost.
Take control of my ears, Lord Jesus
Help me to listen, whatever the cost.

Take control of my feet, Lord Jesus
As I endeavour to walk in Your light.
Take control of my tongue, Lord Jesus
As I endeavour to speak what is right.

Direct me to where I should go, Lord
Direct me to whom I should speak
Direct me along the right pathway
As I endeavour souls to seek.

Teach me to show compassion
Teach me to share others' views
Teach me to be more Christ-like
As I endeavour to spread the 'good news'.

Praise the Lord!

Teressa Rhoden

Carrie

(Is it really better to have loved and lost
than to have never have loved at all?)

When I saw you standing in that crowd
You made my heartbeat stutter
Your smile breathed new life into my world
And set my mind a-flutter

You chased away those looming rain clouds
Made that winter feel like spring
I felt the flowers bloom from 'neath the ground
As birds began to sing

Your blue eyes beamed as brightly as the sun
That rises in the morn
Upon a face that glowed as heavenly pure
As one of God's newborn

And as the wind sailed softly through the trees
Aloft without a care
The sunlight slowly wandered into view
To light your golden hair

So upon reading this I hope you see
The true warmth that you store
A love for which I was so stupid to
Pass up on and ignore

Kevin McNulty

20th September

Peace And Calm

(For my boys, James, Martin, David and John)

Grant to me Your calm
Peace through me to flow
Lord, in this world of plenty
It's all I want to know,
Help me when my head it hurts
When my heart is heavy
If that I should falter Lord
I ask Thou keep me steady.

The gentle power of Your touch
Is to me like balm
Peace it now flows freely
Restored to me all calm.

Mary Thompson

Nothing

Twice nothing is still nothing
So there is nothing gained
Believe in nothing and nothing will happen
And still nothing will be attained

But we aren't put on Earth for nothing
We all have a purpose in life
If it's only to get married and have a husband or a wife
Someone to share your life with - someone with whom you can talk
And when you can no longer run through life
There's a companion with whom you can walk!

But then just like the Trinity most things come in threes
Like Faith, Hope and Charity and the three degrees!
The degree of faith in Jesus - the degree of trust in your Lord
The degree of trust in each other, so that we live in sweet accord
Nothingness will fade away and everything is gained
You've gained your faith, you're filled with hope
Now everything's attained!

Anthony J Gibson

Collections

In winter the old leaf is waiting for nothing
And in waiting the old leaf collects everything.
Through the swirl of the stickiness of snow arriving
Comes its jagged, corniced, personal mountain.
A soundless collection of ice still crystals.
The leaf's collection in an upturned hand;
My minuscule mountain
My corporeal collection
To hold as my treasure until my
Time comes to give back to the sky.

John White

Autumn

The autumn months have now arrived
And garden plants look quite deprived
The air so cool and lack of light
As the shorter day becomes a long night
Crisp golden leaves fall to the ground
To collect and create a mass all around
Work of pruning has to begin
On trees and bushes found within
Being their final trim of the year
As end of growth is now so near
Words in my mind begin to conceive
Of life in the garden I see and believe
I picture scenes of the autumn time
And sentences formed begin to rhyme
'I am the true vine,' is what I perceive
And the true fruit is what I receive
A plantation of such a small seed
And growth overtaking into the lead
Summer has passed and now for a rest
To see what the spring has to show at its best

James Stephen Thompson

24th September

The Way

Be
of faith
all ye
who tread
the mysterious way.
Take with thy heart,
ne'er casting all to just one day.
The way be long,
or,
so they say,
but strive before thee lay.
Dream some dreams,
be strong,
be kind upon thy stay,
then, then,
rest awhile.
Rest awhile and pray.

Diana Mudd

24th September

Peace In Freedom

I lounge, loiter and watch: the world hurries along
To complete its business; a Yellowstone song
Blesses my Sunday of peace.
No cares, okay some, but most left behind
Out of soul, out of body, thrown out of a mind
Emptied - a blissful release.
I have total freedom, well nearly so,
Nothing to phase me, nowhere to go,
Except do just as I please.

Enough cash to spend, enough food to eat,
A Harley to ride, more mothers to meet,
Discuss politics, societal needs
And concerns, unafraid of who hears
Dissent or agreement. To speak without fear
Is precious, not taken with ease
Nor for granted. Falls to the so very few
To have peace in freedom as some of us do,
Not a stifling death-by-degrees.

Reminder to self: take it not as given
But always thank God ensconced in His Heaven
As He blesses this Sunday of peace.

Mark Murphy

25th September

Prayer Power

P rayer from the heart, make time for each day,
R each out and protect, pray all danger away,
A ngels graciously wish to assist and to take
Y our prayers Heavenward safely and never forsake,
E ver-presently watchful, they guide and empower
R esistance to evil, through the strength of prayer power.

P ray morning and night, perfect work is a prayer,
O vercome discontent, pray for peace you can share,
W ars can be averted, through praying nationally,
E ach prayer positive, resonates powerfully,
R endezvous in prayer groups, harmonise prayerfully.

Lorna Troop

25th September

Lemons For Sale

I passed a little sign last week,
'Fresh Lemons Here' it read.
'Leave Coins In Box, I'll Empty It
Before I Go To Bed'.

I looked inside, and sure enough,
There, sitting on the ground,
I saw ten dollars all in coins
With lemons all around.

This wasn't in a country town,
But on a city street,
With people passing back and forth,
And cars, and trampling feet.

Those city folk were honest,
Just as country folk might be.
The owner's trust was well repaid,
And that's what humbled me.

How often do we read of crime
And violence and sin,
But many times we fail to see
That little spark within ...

That little spark which God has put
In every person's mind.
That conscience which enables us
To love and to be kind.

Erica Morley

Autumn

Autumn climax of the year
Sum of all her richest moments
When trees stand rapt in unconsuming flame.
What a clamour of colour
Glowing yellow, copper, red and gold.
Such utter loveliness
Ready for lavishing on the earth below.
Bringing us, however briefly into joy
As we experience the artistry
And infinite variety of nature
In this flame-like wonder.

Idris Woodfield

27th September

Lost In Time

Autumn's magic
Shimmering in gold
Whispers from the leaves
By a love, untold
The magic has gone
Like the band of gold
What happened to the
Love we shared?
Golden moments
As memories 'fall'
Like autumn rain
Faded leaves
From trees in a chill breeze
Like embers from a past
Our September's sad refrain
A golden treasure
From the past.

Margaret Parnell

27th September

Swallow Across The Moon

A late swallow flighting urgently across dusk skies;
a full moon floods a pool of glory behind cloud-bars.
A tiny frog hops where the path gleams after rain.
The child stands enchanted.

'Why?' comes his voice out of silence.
'Why can't I stand here forever, looking at the moon?'

'The moon will move across the sky, sweetheart.'

'Why does it have to move, why do clouds come across it?'

'The wind blows them.'

'Why, why does it blow?
Every time I like something, every time I'm happy,
it changes, it breaks, it moves and goes away.'

'It was always so.
The Greeks said, thousands of years ago,
you cannot step twice into the same river.
The water changes, changes every hour.
And the cry of a bird is once forever;
that bird will never cry that cry again from that perfect place.
But there is another beauty, round the bend of the river.
And who knows,
perhaps Heaven, among other things,
will be going back to visit again the most perfect moments
and able to stay, this time, as long as we like.'

He was silent, looking at the moon.
Then, 'I would stay a thousand years.'

But he shivers, as the night wind bends the grass.
'Come on, my lamb, it's bedtime.
Heaven is not yet. But there are many beauties
and you have a heart to see them, and to love them.
That is a gift. Come on, my lamb, to bed.'

Eve Kimber

Dreaming

(To my beautiful, strong, courageous sister, Lizzy
and my brother-in-law Mark, for his strength of character)

My life has become a lonely one, trusted friends are becoming few,
Being a single parent is hard work and rewarding, but often leaves you blue.
Your life is what you make of it, I am constantly being told,
I have responsibilities, and I'm needed, until I am sold
I don't wish to complain or grumble, of what I could become
I choose to do my role for now, and just dream distant fun
My prince on a white charger will whisk me up and carry me away
Kiss away my troubles and worries which haunt me every day
He will build me a fine castle high upon a mountain top
Then let go of me, and I'll come down with a mighty big plop!
I'll dust myself down once again, and carry on once more
And make my life a happy one, and not a constant chore!

Alison Mitchell

The Cross

When I was a lad of ten or eleven
I went to a market one Saturday morn
And on a stall amidst the stands
I found something shiny and small with my hands.
The price that was asked was all that I had
A sixpence I'd saved from the errands I'd run
I handed it over with never a thought
I'd bought me a cross, a cross I had bought.
I treasured that cross and a present it was
For my dear, dear, mother as she lay in her bed
She smiled as she took it and gave it a kiss
With a tear in her eye and a smile on her face
She left me alone, just me and my cross
It's now my turn to go and I know
She'll be there to welcome me home
With a smile and a tear
But the tear will be joyful
For as you see, I'll be coming home
My cross and me.

R Bateman

30th September

Only A Whisper Away

When your heart is aching
For loved ones who have gone
Do not be disheartened
For their love still lingers on.
It is all around you
In all you say and do
Their presence still surrounds you
And you can start anew.
For love is ever present
It lifts you every day
And although you cannot see them
They're only a whisper away.
Their influence through their lifetime
Is moulded in your soul
You may feel bereft and sad too
But you can still be whole.
Sweet memories can lift your spirit
And help you on your way
Kind deeds and all they stood for
Are only a whisper away.
Your heart can still be strong then
So whatever comes what may
With courage you must go onward
For they're still only a whisper away.
The road may look quite daunting
But feel its sunshine's ray
You're not alone on your journey
They're only a whisper away.

Mollie D Earl

Seascape

Exploring his canvas of unrelieved white
he guided the brush in his hand
to paint iridescence in ultramarine
with flecks of sea danced over land.
His eye understood this incredible scene
of pebbles and glittering sand.

The shadowy background was sombre and dull
but glimmering rays from the sun
shot beams on the crest of a hovering wave
and half-light beneath every one.
A luminous sheen on the billowing deep
enlivened the work he had done.

The artist was reaching the edge of his world
discovering boats on the sea
with shifting reflections in palest of tones
and sails tempestuous and free.
Each stroke of his brush was made with such care
it looked in proportion to me.

Forgetting the patchwork of streaks on himself,
he skillfully laboured all day.
A towering headland soared up to the clouds
in ochre and umber or grey.
Completing a yacht in vermilion and rust
he folded his easel away.

The seascape was mounted and hung on a wall.
When days became longer and cold
he lifted his eyes from the smouldering fire
to travel triumphant and bold
up towering cliffs to the crest of his world.
This picture will never be sold.

Nancy Reeves

You

Rain ran out of stone sky -
a marathon cloudburst.
Your voice caught shards of sun,
arced them into colour.

The fridge was dark and empty -
defrost button working overtime.
You fired the oven,
made a feast out of a famine.

The garden was wild with weeds -
flowers murdered before birth.
You mowed the lawn in stripes,
Drew attention to tilled earth.

The house was a disaster -
falling in disarray and dust.
You swept through with a clean broom,
hoovered up the rest.

My room was dishevelled and cluttered -
with my paintings and books.
You left it, just as it was,
an expression of me and my looks.

Vivien Steels

3rd October

Some Pleasures I Have Known …

To lay upon the golden sand,
Where the waves lap at my feet.
Drinking ice-cold lemonade,
Warmed by the sun's kind heat.
Buried deep amongst the plot
Of some carefully crafted novel.
Away from the bustle of city life
And the crime and grime of that hovel.

Swooping through leaves in autumn time
When the world is draped in gold.
Trudging through the crisp clean snow,
When it's fresh and bitingly cold.
Returning to the inside warmth,
Toasting chestnuts over the fire.
Sharing time with chosen ones,
To the sounds of the Christmas choir.

Alison Adams

4th October

What Will Today Bring?

Another day - what will it bring?
Will I go out? Will I stay in?
If I'm out I see people moving about
If I stop in I see nothing - just chaos and shouts.
I should do 'this and that', I should clear up and cook
But I'd rather sit down and look at a book.
So what shall I do on this special day?
It's my 85th birthday, so I've come a long way.
Some days have been easy, some have been hard,
But I've had folk to help me, they kept me 'on guard'!
One day I shall come to the end of the road,
But I hope it's not yet, I'm not willing to go.
I've enjoyed my life, I'm not near the end,
There is so much to do, so much to tend.
I like being alive to look over the gate
So please God, listen - I'd rather wait.

Doris E Pullen

Lighthouse

In the midst of storm seas
Born from clusters of rocks
I rise tall and white
Scanning the far horizons
Of darkened ocean
Alone amidst hurricanes and typhoons
I watch over the world
Through day and night
So the ships of mankind
Pass safe with my light
I am an outpost of land
Outsider in oceans
Bearing in my stone heart
Secrets of the future

Neil C Roper

5th October

Love Sublime

Whose shadow was always there by my side
        Whenever I was left alone ...
Who would be that flicker of light in darkness
        When every hope was gone ...
For that love sublime ... for that peace
        Is my unending quest ...

Let me believe that the protection of your love
        Is always mine ...
Let me believe that I could always surrender
        Myself at your shrine ...
For that love sublime ... for that peace
        Is my unending quest ...

Like a child hiding his face away from the world
        On his mother's chest ...
He needs to hold his father's little finger
        And those arms to rest ...
For that love sublime ... for that peace
        Is my unending quest ...

Like a bird, lost in the vast blue sky,
        Searching for its nest ...
For that love sublime ... for that peace ...
        Is my unending quest.

Vivek P Sarma

Me! Fight Demons?

In 1 Corinthians Chapter 12,
we learn of spiritual gifts we possess,
but this is no tale of goblin or elf,
rather, war against Satan's minions no less.

I could not face down this deadly foe,
with all his dark power that lies within,
how to stand, I would not know,
afraid and powerless, how could I win!

But an army is not all fighting men,
they need to be fed, transported, equipped,
and back home there are yet more again,
who make weapons which to the front are shipped.

When a spiritual warrior enters Satan's lair,
his armour of God buckled on and true,
the power to win is sacrificial prayer,
his weapons are fully charged by you.

When we use any of God's holy gifts,
preaching, teaching and encouragement too,
spiritual warriors are given a lift,
the power of the Holy Spirit flowing through.

Helping, mercy and faith shine bright,
leadership, management and giving, surge,
flashing like a laser at the speed of light,
turning demonic war songs to a dirge.

In spiritual warfare we stand unified,
all parts of the body working in line,
resurrected in the image of He who died,
the victory over demons is yours and mine.

Bill Hayles

My Everything

Emma you mean the world to me
You're everything I've longed to be

For you there's nothing I won't do
I'd gladly give my life for you

When we first kissed on New Year's Eve
My heartbeat stopped, I couldn't breathe

And it's been like that ever since
You're my princess, I'm your prince

You're my flower, I'm your rain
When we're apart, I share your pain

I dream to wake and see your face
A gentle kiss, a warm embrace

I love it when we sit and talk
And when we hold hands when we walk

I want us to grow old together
I want to be soulmates forever

I want to spend more time with you
It's lovely when it's just us two

I love your eyes, your lips, your touch
Poppet, I'm missing you so much

I watch your face while you're asleep
You dream so softly, angels weep

I love you more than you can tell
My heart's been put under a spell

Without you I am incomplete
A centipede without its feet

I want to live life to the end
Spent with you, my bestest friend

I'll love you to the end of time
From Trev, your loving Valentine

Trevor Reynolds

6th October

Beautiful Morning

I stopped to stare this morning
At what God had given me
No colour television, video or DVD
I was surrounded by beauty
As far as my eyes could see.

The sun was rising in the eastern sky
I could see a bumblebee.

Two collared doves were feeding
As the sun shone brightly down
Its golden rays were shimmering
like gold dust on the ground.

I watched a brood of starlings
Test their wings for the very first time
As a spider weaved its fragile web
Around my washing line.

An orange-tipped butterfly, flitted from nettle to nettle
It landed upon a flower and then decided to settle.

A ladybird walked across the stony path
As a pheasant wandered into view,
Then a tiny frog hopped out the pond
Across the grass covered in dew.

God had given me this moment in time
To cherish and make mine,
Thank You Lord for these things so free,
Their beauty will forever always live with me.

Christine Hardemon

7th October

Church Women

For we are more than teapots after all,
Our produce not confined to church fête stall,
More than sandwich-makers, bakers of cakes ...
We have been present at both birth and death,
Studied philosophy, sung in the choir,
Written poems, read Zen and been on fire
With wonder in the unexpected breath
Of wind at dawn, when watching on our own
After a long night's nursing by some bed:
Practised meditation, been by the Spirit led,
Argued with God, found answers out alone,
Got some things right, seen others as mistakes,
We paint, create, make music; surely we
Must qualify for more than making tea.

Susan Latimer

Hymn To God

'Tis for Thy cause, Thy cause alone
We stand ten thousand souls to win
Ten thousand little ones bought home
From soul-destroying paths of sin.

'Tis for the love that made Thee die
Upon a wooden cross of shame
The Father's will to ratify
The worthy, worthy, worthy lamb.

'Tis for a place in Heaven above
We fight a deathless battle here
A battle not of hate but love
Of Reverence and godly fear.

'Tis for that majestory bright
Begun below, in Heaven above
The blessing of our souls to know
An interest in the Saviour's blood.

Peter Buss

8th October

With Child

Beauty beyond the horizon
Surreal, an angel with child
Love's unspoken volume
Captured by the grace of her smile
Seed of serenity nourished
Cocooned on a pillow of love
An unfinished symphony
The creation of life from true love

Maureen Boyd Joines Anderson

My Higher Power

We were born with a higher power,
a life-force alive, allowing me to thrive,
an intelligence of God thrown down
watching my welfare.

We were born with God,
a power so mysteriously ours,
elusive, all inclusive and loving,
you kept me safe.

We were born with an angel,
devoid of wings but constantly with me,
a higher power of wondering light,
though I felt it.

We were born on the departing way,
what more could I say,
my higher power and I were going away,
to the pleasures of Heaven to play.

Anonymous

. 9th October

May You Find ...

As you are spirit, walk in spirit and truth. May you find the joy of your true self and know peace with yourself. Find your sanctuary within each moment of time, may you live safe and free from harm and, when you journey on, may you find treasured loved ones waiting and know loved ones here will always be bound to you and the created order in love that is in truth.

My blessing

Chiang Yee

Morning Song

As I awake this brand new morn
I look up toward the sky ...
And high above the canopy
I watch the bluebirds fly ...
I feel the cool breeze touch my face ...
And hear the whispering wind
That softly sings of all the gifts
That God has given men.
Are we worthy of these precious gifts
That have been so freely given
By the One who blesses all of life
With the chance for new beginnings?
As I gaze upon these miracles
That God has given me,
I send up praise to Heaven
For this world so bright and free.
My mind is filled with wonder
As my heart finds sweet release ...
For the One who brings me to this place,
Also fills my soul with peace.

Deborah Gail Pearson

10th October

My friends and I are all 70 plus,
Conversation always revolves round us,
About various maladies and aches and pains,
We say, 'Oh, it's much worse when it rains',
Or, 'I can't stand this heat,
It's murder on my aching feet'.

Then someone will say, 'My pills don't suit me,
I'll have to throw them away'.
The chemist's not able to take them back,
It makes us glad we don't have to pay,
Surely, to prescribe just a few would be best,
To help our overstretched NHS.

Conversation then moves to operations,
And how long we have to wait,
And how fearful we are, with hospitals being in such a state.

Another discussion we have is about our own mortality,
So many of our contemporaries are passing away,
We realise we have to face reality,
That we are getting older every day,
So it is better to enjoy our life in every way.

Jean Wood

11th October

Heavenly, Lovely Feelings!

Entered like a thief into my bedroom, slowly but steadily,
Was lukewarm sunlight of the rising sun, majestically,
Spreading its fervour flavour all around,
Like a newly blossomed rose flower spreading its sweet fragrance around!

Following was a blowing of cool breeze, flowing with a glow flawlessly,
Like the flow of water in a river, swiftly,
Blowing up, up and down all over my body,
Touching on all my parts of body, gently and softly,
As if to inject into my veins and brains the drug of laziness deeply,
To prolong my sleep indefinitely!

I felt I was in Heaven, like a saint to have the honours,
To have been showered up with petals of heavenly, lovely flowers,
Dipping me deep and deep in scents and perfumes made out of their perfumery parts,
Drowning me deep down in the holy stream of heavenly, lovely feelings of bliss
and blessings!

I never felt thirst or hunger factually,
What I felt conversely,
Were feelings of fullness and heaviness in my stomach incredibly,
Which readied me up to fly in the sky of uncomfortableness like an overfed amazingly!

In my ecstasy I's not even aware of time flying away from me,
Till my mom came shouting at me,
'Have you not got up yet?
Though the time of the bird of breakfast,
Has already flown away like a punctual aeroplane!'

Davis Akkara

11th October

Precious Memories

A dear grandad you are to me,
a loving man you will always be -
I stand here today with so much pride
wishing you were by my side -
I will play for you with all my heart
your love of life, you played your part.

Debbie Evans

12th October

Holidays

I rode the hairy donkeys on the strand
And watched eternal wavelets ebb and flow
And curdle round my pink exploring toes,
Then built ephemeral castles in the sand.
I plunged and swallowed, joyfully afraid,
And shivered in the ocean's cold embrace,
The salty water stung my sunburnt face.
How could I know all this would shortly fade?
Today we sat in comfort on the pier,
Then hand in hand we strolled among the rocks,
We smiled and said we'd come again next year
And patiently wrung out our soaking socks.
So softly home we went and understood
The trade of youth for age is fair and good.

Ruth Blaug

Reflections

Morning light, morning bright,
God's gift to humans
Yet another day of life,
What to do, happiness to bring,
Or is it sadness, sorrow, bombs or
Those in far-off countries starving?

Anniversaries, weddings, life newborn,
All these everyday events,
Families happy for loved ones,
Others living with the ghosts of past traumas,
Bring back 'Candle In The Wind',
God forgive us our many sins.

Music stills unhappy souls,
Heals the tormented, the sadness,
In the gardens flowers bloom,
Happy children laugh and play,
Gloom not a partner for many,
But in far-off lands drought and starvation.

Can there be belief in global warming?
Can we hope the terror will stop?
Can we still have faith in the Almighty?
Do we believe in Man's survival?
What of our many aspirations and dreams?
Can we find solutions, can the situation be redeemed?

Elizabeth Hiddleston

13th October

The Wonders Of The World

The Lord does wonders
Miracles every day
Babies being born
Every hour, every day.

Sunsets over valleys
Wind whips down the brae
People saved from hunger and pain
Provisions sent every day.

The Lord provides
And the Lord taketh away
Who decides to show the way
Take me where the angels play.

Donna Hardie

14th October

He Will Keep The Promise

Looking at the plight of my homeland as it descends into lawlessness,
Leaves me feeling hopeless and dejected, though I remain faithful in prayer.
Two hundred years of struggle and more bad than good tends to happen.
Excessive and uncaring governments have left the people destitute.
Yet my heart is full of thanksgiving, because I believe in a promise,
Given long ago to a man of God, which I claim for myself.
In spite of the obvious, I am confident that He will keep His word.
My country shall rise from the ashes, as the Israel of the olden days.
For like the prophet I know that I have found favour in His sight,
And for my sake, the healing shall surely come to my native soil.

Gladys Bruno

14th October

Let's Say A Prayer

Let's say a prayer for humanity
Let's say a prayer for us all
Let's say a prayer for love and peace not hate and fear and war
Let's say a prayer for the rivers
Let's say a prayer for the seas
Let's say a prayer for the meadows
Let's say a prayer for the trees
Let's say a prayer for all kinds of life on land, in sky, in seas
Let's say a prayer to everything from all humanity.

Greeny

15th October

Awe And Apathy: A Matter Of Perspective

The huge tree stands rock-like,
Overlooking the darkening valleys.
Its limbs are unmoving and its body silent,
As if the scene below is unworthy of any recognition.
Its regularity of occurrence is so familiar it goes hardly noticed.
The tree's stillness reveals a tedium, an indifference and
An unwillingness to acknowledge its surroundings.

A lone man stands beneath the tree's apathy.
His limbs are unmoving,
His body silent.
He stands rock-like.

He hears a faint mechanical clatter bring
The night warming meal to cattle.
Gentle clucks begin to settle into sleep.
The occasional chirp of a nesting bird twitters through the fading day.
A moth begins to dance to the nocturnal music
With the tree's magnificence as a back drop.

The sky begins to glitter with faint twinkles.
A wafting chill tickles the man's skin.
Fresh cleanness fills his lungs with beauty.
A sparkling sharpness tangs on his tongue.
His cluttered thoughts disappear as darkness
Slowly wraps the world in peace.

A lone man stands beneath the tree's apathy.
His limbs are unmoving,
His body silent.
He stands rock-like in awe.

Keith Wright

16th October

Don't Let Sorrow Wail Thee Down

Each day a reason to fly birds find,
They never untune their songs with pains of the mind.
Sun will not stay an extra hour for a saddened face,
Nor moon a little longer for a toil-worn man grace.

Awake brother! Awake and shake off thy tired frown,
What is true joy but to comprehend life's ups and downs,
For there is no fertile ground that will not grow weed,
And no truly fulfilled man that has no need.

Oritsegbemi Emmanuel Jakpa

17th October

My Lips Ran Away With My Voice Box

In a corner of a world,
Where I cannot find peace,
Tears fall from my eyes.
My lips ran away to Greece.

They took my voice box
As a lip gloss bag.
I sit whilst the world mocks,
Labelled useless by a shopping tag.

See I'm very sorry
And hope they understand,
I received a hostage note,
Asking for a grand.

So I decided to pay them,
'Cause I need to be heard.
I handed over a Boots voucher,
I know this sounds absurd.

I tried to bribe them
With lipstick and anti-smoking.
Yet they were so stubborn,
They thought I was joking.

So I cried and I begged
But I could not speak.
And without my energy
They were getting weak.

They made me promise,
Something strange indeed,
To scream and shout,
I jumped and agreed.

Christina Earl

God's Creatures

The sheep were grazing in the field
And rabbits playing and having fun
The cows were sheltering under the trees
To escape the heat of the sun
Horses led from stables for a ride
And dogs taken for a walk on a lead
Pigs eating out of a trough
As chickens waited for their feed
Cats chasing birds on the grass
Then laying down for a sleep
A hedgehog strolling down the path
On his way to the dung heap
Bees flitting from flower to flower
Gathering the pollen for their hives
Varied butterflies flying around
For in nature there are many different lives
As God made this world for us all
Both humans and creatures big and small.

Diana Daley

Realisation

I am looking in the mirror now
And wondering what is wrong
I don't see myself in there anymore
I wonder where I have gone
I try to think just when it was
The last time that I was there
I've gone and lost myself again
And have been too busy to care.

I don't remember disappearing
I can't remember coming back
But it just goes to show
That you never can know
If it is memory that you lack.

I think I've been here all along
But never noticed that it was me
Or maybe I went blind for a while
And forgot that I could see
It could be that there is no one here
To tell me who to be ...

I need to find myself again
I need to be the one
To tell myself
To sort me out
To try and get things done.

It is time to waken up now
Time to start anew
To find a new reflection
And to find a better view.

I promise this
I will not miss
My old one when I do.

Emma Jane Glenning

19th October

Revelation

Beauty and certainty
Give us good cheer
Come fill me with love
For being right here
Comfort is sure
Where angels fly
Joy rule our hearts
And never ask why
Here for the living
As life is our way
So go on enjoy it
Be here for today.

Deborah Hall

Westminster Abbey, 19th October, 2004

My old college! King's, in London!
Now 175 years of age
Celebrates its lovely Christian heritage
And a dazzling fanfare of trumpets proclaims
  The Princess Royal's arrival!

She reads the Declaration of King George IV,
Announcing that love and learning are inseparable -
Christianity puts the clear blessing on learning;
  Amen, amen.

Later just after the service, one old scholar
(Another Alumnus!) remarks,
'It's good to belong to something!' and smiles.

Still later, over in the Strand, I seek (in vain)
My old literary links, and try to find
The Rhymers' Club place near that street;
The Cheshire Cheese of William Butler Yeats.

Mike Green

20th October

Happiness

To open up my eyes at early light of dawn
And hear birds' chorus, greet the summer morn
Turn to see my husband sleeping, warm
Is happiness.

A grandchild's sticky hand, trusting, clenching mine
To wash those grubby knees, remove the grime,
His face lights up when ticking clock does chime,
That's happiness.

The sound of the voice of my son from overseas,
The tang of ozone borne on a salty breeze
Fresh fish with chips and mushy peas,
That's happiness.

Family photographs taken long ago
Fond memories of holidays, frolics in the snow
Today the caring love they ever show,
Brings happiness.

Sunday morning service, voices raised in praise
The time to ponder, reflect and maybe change your ways,
Smiles from friends as around the church I gaze,
Is happiness.

Pamela Carder

20th October

The Little Things

When we hurt in times of pain
And I feel the pouring rain
Fall upon me, shall I complain?
Because I won't remember
No I won't remember
Little things I knew
Who will pull me through?

Will I walk this path alone
Without you to guide me on
Be my strength and keep me strong?
Because I don't remember
No I don't remember
Little things you'd do
Who will see me through?

Watch the candle in the dark
Dance like beating hearts
We shall meet and we shall laugh
Because I do remember
Yes I do remember
Little things you'd do
When I think of you
You pull me through.

Jacqueline Taylor

21st October

Thoughts Stirred From Sleeplessness

It could be past midnight but I would still settle here,
Your head sat neatly in the cradle of my arms.
The minutes would pass silently, followed only by the
Rising of your hair upon my chest. I would watch the
Night become tomorrow and in the morning
Watch you wake from gentle rest.

It could be colder than winter but I would still settle here,
Setting the covers to keep you warm. The clouds may form
Outside, but for now we are inside and away from harm.
I would bow to kiss your head and perhaps you would
Rise with the sun the next morning, the embrace still
Set in your memory.

It could be darker than thunder but I would still settle here,
Lighting small candles like stars brought in from the sky.
As you dream I would wonder what thoughts would pass
Through your mind; our shadows dancing upon the walls.
The scent of vanilla floats in the air, and in the morning
Wish for another peaceful day.

D Wakefield

Eternity With God

Eternity with God
As He your Maker
Will lead you to glory
From the day of birth
Through all your days on Earth.

With life's sadness and tears
Filled with fears.
Reach now for those golden years
You will then understand
All life's pressures at hand.

Eternal life filled with joy and laughter
Through Earthly life, to journey's end
Archangels, then will ascend
For this is the beginning my friend.

John Robinson

Lyrical Minds

Some people live with a song in their heart
And an anthem of hope in their soul,
Blessed with the gleam of a musical theme,
To rhyme all these dreams is their goal.

These are the folk with the lyrical minds,
Whose words make a beautiful sound,
To send us each day, to sing and to play,
The sweet notes that make life go round.

Let's all give thanks for the song and the dance,
The melodies we love to hear,
The teenage romance that begins with a glance,
The heartbreak that brings on a tear.

So, who are these folks with the lyrical minds?
They're poets, like you and me,
Who write lines of love, with some help from above,
Sharing laughter and glad company.

Brenda Maple

Make It

The decision is there to be made; the deed requires to be done,
The life has just got to be lived; the battle needs to be won.
There's no use bemoaning your fate
Or thinking you're going to die,
Of course we know sometime you are, but why not give living a try?

Come strengthen the sinews of hope, gird up the loins of your mind,
See how you've managed this far; remember all that's behind.
The past has prepared you for now
But this is the present, my friend,
So make up your mind to go on, and stick with it right to the end.

Believe me the best is to come, you haven't seen half of it yet!
You're older and weaker maybe, though wiser as well don't forget.
So screw up your courage, old son,
Make that decision to fight,
And don't give it up till you've won, for that way the future is bright.

Ray Smart

24th October

Put On The Whole Armour Of God

You need a breastplate
To repel the fiery dart.
Righteousness is needed
To protect your heart.
But yours is only filthy rags;
Wear His!
It's clean and pure,
And with it you'll be able to endure.

The shield of faith
You need to take upon your arm,
For Satan always tries
To knock you down and do you harm.
Don't let him win!
Be strong!
God's word is always right
And Satan's wrong.

Your head will need protection.
For you, Christ dearly won
The helmet of salvation.
Put it on!
Then wear the belt of truth,
And wield your sword.
Stand in God's power and pray,
And trust His word.

Shirley Ballantine

24th October

Upon Reflection - Quiet Scandal

Reflection always twists the truth,
Memory of magic days of youth,
And so-called friends who never were.
Illusions. The love - was never there

Under quiet's candlelight, the glow
In levels of ourselves we do not know
In rooms within, in depths unused
Events in mystery become suffused

To cycle back as pleases it to do
In iterations we call me and you
Ourselves we know the least of all
That quiet scandal hid behind a wall.

Who knows what processes arcane
Dominate in this realm of sane
Or mad or bad - what labels we apply
For every day I'm born and also die.

Eric McCrossan

Gold In A Furnace

Tested as gold in a furnace
Thus the true mettle is found,
The strength of the heat shows the strength of the gold
It proves that the substance is sound.

If the metal is base it will weaken
And lose its full strength in the blast.
Tin, copper and lead will melt and give way,
Only the gold will stand fast.

The mettle of true faith is precious
Like gold it's eternal and pure,
Doubt and despair will vanish like wax
And the gold that's true faith will endure.

M Dawson

26th October

Keep Smiling Through

A smile helps you on your way,
It helps to brighten up your day,
A smile lifts the spirits,
A smile carries love,
It makes one feel special
Like a blessing from above,
It breaks down many barriers
Of culture and of creed.
You could succeed in doing
What politicians cannot do,
Contributing towards a peaceful world,
So start afresh, each day is new.

Rachel E Joyce

26th October

Serenity

Serenity ...
What a tranquil place,
the morning light
with all promise awakens.
This day to be handled with grace.
Grace ...
is the knowing
the showing of love
to yourself and all others.
While quietly saving within a space
to travel life at a healthy pace.

For each day's journey
encompasses the need
to value life's treasures.
'What are they?' you say.
Well often they are lost
in the material shuffle;
success is not what to possess
but oh the enrichment
- the feeling serene
when grace is your charm
and rich in your friends
- that cushion between.

Wilma G Paton

27th October

As A Man Thinks So He Is

The mind carves a road in the future.
Fields of hope's corn and the wheat of purity are ripe for picking.
Their yellow summer smile feeds the soul.

Dare not to glance back.
Your heart turns to salt; your feet sink in quicksand.
Despair will suffocate your soul.

Nor run hastily into the future.
Fear's vicious snare will crush life.
Its jaws will ruthlessly pulp your heart.

Today's journey has its ruts and boulders,
But fear not.
Look up as you travel,
The valley of the shadow of death is passable.
Whistle the melody of the Homeland,
A song of life and joy.

Know you are a traveller on this road:
A traveller heading home.

Ruth M Ellett

Heaven Awaits!

O how can words translate the fullness of God?
'Holy, Holy, Holy is the Lord'
The glory, the splendour, the majesty, the power
For Thine is the kingdom
Exalted, enthroned
Sovereign, unlimited
All encompassing, crowned.

I'm drawn to the throne to join heavenly host.
No longer one so wearied and worn
But a creature who's shed its restrictive cocoon
Standing flawless and bold
Complete and adorned
In the beauty and radiance
Of the Father's perfect love.

God Himself is with us, union sweet.
Contentment, peace, fulfilment deep
Like the wonder of cradling your newborn babe.
The thrill of communion
As saints celebrate
Inexplicable bonds.
The lion lies with the lamb.

Surrounded by beauty so pure and immense
Creation conceives a perfection
Which glistens in the glory of His presence.
So vibrant in colour,
Ablaze and intense.
Timeless apparel which
Transcends magnificence.

Rachel Hall-Smith

28th October

Rain

The heavy patters of the rain
It hits the tin again, again,
But still the silence is such bliss
'Cause quietness comes along with this.
This silence but not fright,
That we hear alone at night.
So savour this quiet thought with me,
That this is a nice place to be.

Eleanor Anderson

Uplift

On your feet
Look neat
On the street
At early morning call
Mass in the past
Seven just before work
Happenings all through the night
Out of luck
Phone Uncle Buck
Send me your pillow to dream on
Schemes and scenes
Beg, borrow or steal
Tomorrow is mine
Hold life in your hand
Be grand
Sending messages good or true
Blue mood I am in
Colour me beautiful
Fending for yourself
Ask another question
Answers locked up
In a drawer in a desk
Somewhere in the Foreign Office
Foreign people write
About light and dark
Night or day
Sing away until early morn
Catch the Midnight Express
Uplifting emotions
A cloud of knowing uplifting feeling

S M Thompson

30th October

It was quiet and still in the room, the silence
only broken by the ticking of the clocks;
accepting every hour when one by one
they chimed in orderly succession.
Away from busy traffic, ringing phones and faxes,
at last retirement brings a peace so ably earned.
Now, no demanding, petulant public,
just a quiet companion lying at my feet.
Time now for rambling leafy walks,
and sunny afternoons about the garden.
But age has come to him more quickly,
as canine years, so short to human time,
have slowed his legs and left him breathless,
to stand and watch the rabbits he'd once chased,
frolic across the fields in gay abandon.

But now the quietness holds an empty sadness.
No soft warm body sleeping on the mat.
No longer heard the steady rhythmic breathing.
No more the patter of feet upon the tiles.
No other dog could ever take his place.
No other dog could look with those deep eyes,
not only understanding every word,
but knowing too, my feelings and my thoughts.
I never thought so small a living creature
could take a place so vast within my heart.

Maureen Powell

Saving Grace

When days are long and times are tough
You feel that life's thrown quite enough.
Take a rest, sit down a while, remember how it feels to smile.

A minute may be all it takes for a saving grace to light your face
Do not fret, even if it's short and strained
A little happiness is what you have gained.

If the gloom should keep you down
Don't lose your smile or start to frown
There'll always be a brighter way
To end your troubles and start the day.

Marie Butler

To Dani

You humble me,
Within a chuckle,
Safe in my arms,
So small yet holding power,
To frighten me ... overrule me
Nothing hurts like your tears.

I am lost in middle age,
Fear, insecurity and doubt,
Until you embrace, trust and love me,
Unable to judge me.

Knowing when I breathe my last,
You will not understand,
But wonder and ask why,
The man I remember vaguely,
The fool who entertained me,
Where has he gone?

Norman Dickson

2nd November

Thought For The Day

Never rush into tomorrow
We don't know what's in store
Savour the moments that pass each day
And enjoy them evermore.

When bad days come
And life muddles by
Remember the sunshine
And look to the sky.

For when your sky is clear
And the clouds roll away
Remember the good times
And enjoy the day.

Ruth Clarke

Falling Leaves

The grey November sky above my head,
The fallen leaves about my feet,
The year is dying.
Yet deep within that death
There lies a hope, new life.

I stoop and take a fallen leaf,
Brittle and brown between my fingers,
It crumbles into tiny fragments
Falling to the earth, there to merge
With its dark moist substance.

As winter spreads its frosty coating
Deep down those million leafy fragments
Enrich life-giving soil
Till in the warmth of spring
Green shoots will spear towards the sun.

Our lives are like the fallow earth,
We need to take within ourselves
The teaching and the love of our dear Lord.
We, too, may come to a new spring,
Our dead lives waking to a glorious future.
Just as from His rocky tomb
Our Lord in springtime came
Alive and vibrant, risen from the dead.

Take up a dead, dry leaf and look at it,
And it can teach us all we need to know,
Our faith no longer will be dead.

Roma Davies

4th November

The Night Candle Flower

(Translated from Hebrew by Linda Zisquit)

All the questions bloom at night
Who and what is 'me'?
Where is the army of dead?
Is Man really above the beast?
Why is so much blood shed?
Who has the power to fix this world?
Who will love me here and beyond?
All the questions
Like a night candle
Blown out in the light
My shore is filled with flowers
That only bloom at night.

Nava Semel

Bonfire Night

The bangs deafening, flames flicker and dance,
The night sky aglow with an orange light,
Around the bonfire, happy children prance,
Showers of golden rain fall through this night.
Guy Fawkes sits aloft on his burning throne,
The crackling embers glow red beneath him,
Hand-held sparklers make patterns of their own,
Dazzling fireworks transform a night once dim.
November the sixth dawns cold and dreary,
Debris scattered, firework tubes damp and dead,
Once bright sparkler wands left black and wiry,
Charred embers cindery, no longer red.
Last night, explosive excitement around,
Today, a dark sooty patch marks the ground!

Pat Heppel

It's Something

It's something to know,
When the east wind blows
That the sky behind is blue,
Though the storm drive fast,
It will end at last and the
Sun comes shining through.
It's something to keep
When the snow lies deep,
One's heart and spirit in tune,
To be sunny and true
The whole year through
In November as well as June.
It's something to stand,
To work on the land
And carry the share of the load,
To keep up the pace,
With a smile on your face
When we come to the uphill road.

Edward Brookes

Source

I light the touchpaper
Then stand well back
Still I am covered in sparks
They reach me from miles away
On track
Again I am showered
With dancing darts of fire
I cling to their tails
Travelling back
To their source
They take me
Straight to You
You answer my prayer
My Lord
No other way will do.

Glenda Stryker

Trust

Don't fear.
Don't fret.
Trust.

Don't worry.
Don't cry.
Trust.

Don't run.
Don't hide.
Trust.

Be strong.
Be wise.
Trust.

Be at peace.
Be happy.
Trust.

Be calm.
Be alive.
Trust.

Like a brother.
As a friend.
Trust.

To your Lord.
Give your life.
And trust.

Anne Marie Latham

O Lord my God I joyfully
Will praise His name each day
And to the great exalted One
To You I'll humbly pray
When out of Zion You were there
To lead Your people free
We look again to You oh Lord
A peaceful land to see

For to each one a helping hand
And wars forever cease
Your nature's beauty given to us
Your beauteous land at peace
Oh Lord we thankfully will see
Space for each one to live
And bread of life from You oh Lord
Will to Your people give

For great You are above all things
Forgiving You will be
Our many sins will not account
A joyful Earth we'll see
Euodia and Syntyche
And all the world around
At peace at last with You oh Lord
Will praise with joyful sound

Mary Hudson

8th November

Reach For My Hand

When darkness comes into your life,
And all around you see despair,
Don't worry, don't cry, just reach for my hand,
Because I will always be there.

When misery has you in its grasp,
And you feel like you can't go on,
My hand will be there to steady you,
Reach out, and I'll help you along.

Reach out, reach out, reach out for my hand,
Don't look back, and never give in,
For as long as I hold your hand in mine,
The pain will be gone, replaced by the love held within.

Pete Robins

9th November

Songbird, high up in the tree,
Sing a little song for me,
Sing a song of God's creation,
Sing a song of exaltation!
Sing your song and sing it loud.
Sing it long and sing it proud,
Come sing, sweet songbird, in your tree,
And let your music set me free.

Kevin Baskin

9th November

Thoughts From God's 'Potting Shed'

Put God's serenity clause in your life.
Come from the rush-dash syndrome into the
'I shall listen to You, Father,
Cause me to be aware of Your footstool.
Help me understand the need of rest.'
Be adorned with Christ's blessings,
Don't become impoverished.
God wants to lavish gifts on you.
Come, visit His storehouse -
Sink to swim,
Run to win;
Don't drown by being at odds with yourself.
Enjoy being alive 'in Christ'.
Fellowship with Him, harmonise with Him.
Get used to wearing His security blanket!
Test the obvious - prayerfully converse the rest,
Seeking out the motivation, going beyond the obvious.
Take to looking for tasks that may be ahead.
Christ is not a steam-roller,
His patience with you is so protective yet
At the same time is so challenging;
Rather like the protective coating on a seed
Which ensures it grows as well as providing
The tender, loving care it so needs.
So be challenged.

Anne Hadley

10th November

Reflection Of The Night

My dear, last night, whilst dreaming
You came back to me
Many years had rolled away
We were young and free
We sat so close together
Your lips caressed my face
The magic aura of it all
Could have set the world ablaze
You gave that certain smile of yours
Which could melt the coldest heart
Brushed my hair with tenderness
As the tears began to start
We walked through streets of yesterday
Relived the joys we knew
Travelled through our lifetime
Before the night was done

Then I awoke to daylight and found myself alone
I'd dreamed our life away
You had found a new abode
The final choice one has to make
Being neighbour to the Lord
God bless

Mary V Ciarella Murray

11th November

By Strawberry Hill On Remembrance Day

Through Clevedon's valley, this bright November morn
I walk in peace past All Saints' Church
Which nestles cosy in this place
Among the bronze and gold of windswept trees
Whose leaves now torn from branch by breeze
Great gusts that whistle by
Church spire peaks high in the air
Fine welcome to this place of prayer.
As proud she stands like solid rock
Whilst chiming out her peal of bells
And calling to her passing flock
Come in for prayer and wish-you wells.

By Strawberry Hill, our rugged cross
Set back on roadside – quiet spot
For passers-by to pause a while
Reflection time, remembrance plot.

The blood-red wreath of poppies lie
For those who gave themselves, and died
They fought for right ... life ebbed away,
We thank them this Remembrance Day.

Lynda Arnold

11th November

Tranquillity

All the happenings in the world today
Thrust thy soul upon the Lord
When thou will not stray
But forever feel in accord

Thou will find tranquillity
In every hour awake
Where'er thou may be
Finding life to explore and create

As each day passes by
One seeks sanctuary
Which seems forever nigh
But one can find tranquillity

The Lord be forever near
To show thee the way
It is very clear
With blessings every day

Thou feel not forsaken
Seeking the Lord spiritually
As thou feel taken
Into a world filled with tranquillity

A light within burns bright
That you offer to folk passing by
So they may feel the light
Taking away all sigh

Thrust thy soul upon the Lord
Be there forever tranquillity
For thou be with nature in accord
Surrounded by all the world's beauty.

Amelia Petherick

Eternal Optimism

To open each service the vicar would start
By thanking the Lord from the depths of his heart.
His amazed congregation could never be sure
What new things each week he would thank the Lord for,
But they knew beyond doubt, just as night follows day,
That he'd thank Him for something, for that was his way.

One terrible Sunday a storm had set in
And the vicar arrived looking soaked to the skin.
He won't offer thanks for today, people thought,
For once in his life the old devil's been caught!
But the vicar arose and he started to pray
Saying, 'Thank God that most days are not like today.'

Alan Millard

12th November

I Know

You know, I really do mean it
When I say I know how you feel
I do know what you're going through
Is painful and very real.
I know you're not exaggerating
Or pretending in any way
It really is a trying time
Getting harder every day.
I do know what you're going through
As I have been there too
And time right now just brings you pain
There seems like no let up for you.
I won't pretend it's easy
You'll cope in your own way
You take your time - go at your own pace
And take things day by day.
I know this seems unreal now
But things will improve, it's true
Step by step, you'll smile again
With each day that is new.

Joanne Hale

Is There ...

A pot of gold under
A rainbow sky?
If so, where and why?
For we need no gold
Look up to the magic
We can see but not hold!
So many times in this world
Speak of material greed.
The rainbow of course
Can be explained
But I would rather
Make believe ...
It's magic made in Heaven
With unicorns, Pegasus and all.

M Osmond

14th November

Do You Tell

If your friend is taken for a ride,
Do you tell?
If his heart is sure for breaking,
Do you tell?

When gossips run a story just for fun,
Do you tell?
If his end is in the making,
Do you tell?

When he's all alone and hurting,
Will you stay?
When his every thought is sadness,
Will you stay?

As you watch his heart breaking,
Will you stay?
When the tears are strong and flowing,
Have you love?

When all his fears are showing,
Have you love?
When your friend is all alone,
Have you love?

Do you tell, have you love, will you stay?
Yes, promise him, you'll never go away.

Duchess Newman

14th November

Perfect Dreams

Dream a dream
A perfect dream
Of playing in a ball pit
Or eating ice cream

Quick, fall asleep
Sense a vision so strong
Of memories of a birthday
Or a childhood song

Christmases with family
Everyone's attending
In dreams; that happiness
Is never ending

Playing a game
Like pass the parcel
Or playing with friends
On a big bouncy castle

Dream a dream of
Days with Mum and Dad
A place where you're happy
No need to be sad

Your very own swimming pool
Or days of snow and ice
A perfect dream for every night
Now wouldn't that be nice.

Dan McPheat

15th November

Be Still

Help us to understand
The situations that are out of our hands.
Do we fight on and endeavour to be strong?
We feel so helpless.
Can we see it through.
Are You there for us?
What are we to do
No one on Earth can help.
There is nothing they can do.
We have no one to turn to.
There is only You.
We hear Your words,
'Be still and know that I am God'.
What else can we do, but be still.
We are nothing.
We are Yours alone.
Help us to be strong, to carry on.
To be still and trust in Your will.
Amen.

Patricia M Farbrother

30

... my special birthday present
unwrapped, day by day
and undiminished

no bows to peel with airy fingers
no box to sneak a tempted peek
tingles of a love-struck moment

heaven-sent
on my day of one year older
tasty, flavour-filled
like a candle-topped cake

my flame all fiery
my passion-burning beauty
and sensuous saviour
touching flesh and nimble knowing

exquisite, shining, irresistible
my blonde-locked beauty

nestled, bed-hugged, warm
wrapped close
awakening eyes, touching toes
my wants and dreams and

needs and wishes
she's worshipped, gorgeous
sweet, delicious
... my special birthday present

Jamie Caddick

17th November

Open Up Your Heart

(Dedicated to Mary Clarke, 1808-1902)

When doubt and fear does enter the mind
Answers to questions pounding there one cannot find,
Not knowing how or where a solution will start
It is then I run to you, dear friend, to pen up my heart.

'Tis only you in all this world I found a friend to trust
Knowing you will never betray a confidence, or be unjust,
Counselling my tears you gently take my hand
Then whisper words that say you understand,
Your wisdom gives me faith to start again
This love you show for me takes away my pain.

My life would not be blessed by what you do,
If it were not for my sincere trust in you,
The softness in your eyes helps me in this life to live
And your friendship to me does such pleasure give,
I only ask of life that we will never part
For you are the friend to whom I will open up my heart.

John Clarke

A Smile

Smile and the whole world
Smiles with you
Is a saying since
I don't know when
There is far too much sadness
All over the world
A smile can bring
Comfort no end
If you're down you'll find
It's quite an effort
But then think of happier times
It's uplifting and it will be worth it
A smile brings sun into your life
So come on now
Try a bit harder
If you give a smile
You'll get one back
And that bumpy old world
Will look brighter
Before you know
It will smile back

Jeanette Gaffney

19th November

Happiness Outside Your Door

So much to make you gloomy now
With news of murder and of war
But listen for the lighter tune
Of happiness outside your door

What happened that was nice today?
A letter maybe made you laugh
A blackbird on your window sill
A neighbour waving from the path

Thinking pleasant thoughts can help you
Push the grey ones to one side
Just looking at the family photos
Can fill a heart with smiles of pride

People, pets, relations, babies
A gentle touch from loving wife
Sometimes laughter, sometimes sadness
All give richness to one's life

Norma Griffiths

19th November

Ascent From Resentment

Feeling torn apart, very pulled down,
No room for a smile beneath this heavy frown.
Why do I get so low? So close to the floor,
I kick myself around, then do it some more.

I am my worst enemy during this descent,
Bathe myself in my own resentment.
It's only when I'm almost below the ground,
That I try to stop the punishing sound.

The helping signal arrives just in time,
I hear a saving voice which sounds like mine.
The words encourage me to rise,
But I'm nowhere near reaching the skies.

'Pull yourself together, lift yourself up,
Take the charm of life from your own loving cup.
You've been so unkind to yourself, have to be good!
You can be nice now, as all men should.'

There's a reward for all those who try,
To start the ascent, to give the reply.
To be a whole soul again is my intent
And I begin by burying my resentment.

Alan Bruce Thompson

20th November

Have Faith

When others bring you sorrow
And you are doubting too,
Have faith, my friend, have faith
In everything you do.

For, though unhappy, sad or moaning
And nothing stops those tears from flowing,
Just say it loud, 'I'll keep on going!'
Have faith, my friend, have faith.

When you're sincere, it's very true
That better things will come to you,
So carry on with that belief,
Have faith, my friend, have faith.

And when you're happy, glad you're living,
Your heart is full and all-forgiving,
Then thank the Lord for now you're smiling!
Have faith, my friend, have faith.

Maggie Cartridge

21st November

Trust In The Lord

Cast your cares upon the Lord for He alone is our rock,
A refuge in times of trouble, He stands at the door and He knocks.
For all who will receive Him He comes and sups with him.
Very soon all your fears will seem as nothing, and will fade and grow dim.
Just trust in Him in your time of trouble for He will see you through,
For even though your friends may fail you, He alone cares for you.
Though the turmoil you go through may be long and never seem to end,
Just call on Him, trust in Him, and His Spirit He will send.
For He came as a light into the world to show Man the way,
A way out of the darkness and into the light of day.

Anna Powell

My Final Ave

Mary, my mother, on that day
May my prayer, my final Ave
Be heard by you in Heaven above
And conveyed to the Father with maternal love
Stay close by me at my demise
From Earthly life to Paradise
On this last journey be my guide
And welcome me with arms held wide
United then in joy so sweet
Kneeling humbly at your feet
I to you my Heavenly Mother pray
Please hearken to my last Ave.

Brenda W Hughes

23rd November

Let His Love Shine Through

When called upon to do several humdrum things, like polishing a floor
Or giving some extra help to someone who cannot do their chore
I cannot take the credit for any good that comes out of this!
For the idea wasn't mine in the first place, that nothing should go amiss
All that we do, all that we say
Are orders with which we have been blessed!
Commands are given to be obeyed -
Not ever to be suppressed!
For God is like another person at the end of a telephone line,
Planning and telling us our every move -
With a love that is so Divine.
So, if the Spirit of God shines through,
In everything that I do,
Then take it as a Special Gift
God intended just for you!

M Ross

Poetic Answers

When you have something on your mind and you want to let it out,
Just think about it for a while, what's this problem about?
If you find it won't go away and the anguish is getting worse
Just get a pad and write it down, then put it into verse
Not only will it ease your mind, but stimulate your thought
To show the problem as it is, give answers that you sought
When you have finally worked it out and your mind is now at peace
The anger in you should subside and will eventually cease
If you feel the need to send this message far and wide
Put your poetry into print so others can decide.

David Cameron

Hope lies in black furrowed fields that
Turn lace green in spring.
It's heard over peaty moorland tracks
When skylarks sing
In summer's sun and soars amongst
The stunning scales of 'Ode to Joy'
A symphony of the soul.
Hope comes from the bleat of newborn lambs
On snow-flecked fells.
It's there on every rising sun
On every Chelsea morning
Amongst the snowdrops and crocus of raw winter.
In the words 'You are clear'
In the words 'I love you'
Deeper than Ground Zero
The harvest of faith
The flowers of the forest.

Hayes Turner

26th November

Do You Believe In Magic?

Do not doubt
That in some faraway place
Great magic is being performed on your behalf

That the dark times that you have lived through
Are behind you
Now the sunshine is back in your life

Look to the window
Beneath which prayers were said
To bring luck and blessings into your house

And if you believe in magic
Like a ring bathed in moonlight
Fill each room with it

And with strange and simple words
Fill each breath with it

Doug Cairns

Lifelines

Life is a gift we must accept
And live the life we're given.
A sign of God's eternal love
Bequeathed to us from Heaven.
We all have times of sadness
When sorrow passes by.
To walk the path of grief and pain
We often wonder, *why?*
But by His healing presence
God sends our tears away
And gives us strength and courage
To meet a brighter day.
The greatest joy that life can hold
Is when love comes along.
To live a life with love in it
Makes every day a song.
A caring, sharing, loving heart
The way to live aright
Can chase away life's doubts and fears
And make the spirit bright.
Yes, life's a mix of all these things
There's choices to be made.
To trust Our Lord to guide us through
And not to be afraid.
And when life's span is over
May we in one accord
Pass through the Realms of Rapture
Returning to Our Lord.

Enid Rathbone

Verdi's Requiem, 27th November 2004 St James' Church, Sussex Gardens, London

Alessandro Manzoni fell one day,
His death then a catalyst for the score,
Verdi's great masterpiece, his best I'd say,
We sat in the front row, simply in awe.
The Ingemisco is always haunting,
The beautiful church was both full and warm,
The voices so soft, then loudly booming,
With much moving music, magic was born.
The singing sent such shivers down my spine,
'The wondrous sound of the trumpet rings through',
Grant them rest, and let perpetual light shine,
For Libera Me, I was in tears too.
My diagnosis was two years ago,
Cancer now gone, I love God and life so.

Mary May Robertson

Live Every Moment

Live every moment of your life
As though it were the last
There may be grey clouds in the sky
But they will soon go past
The sunshine will come flooding thro'
And take you by surprise
The beauties of this wondrous world
Will be seen before your eyes
But if those eyes be tear-stained
Or your mind does not receive
The message of its beauty
Or you just cannot believe
That life can be so wonderful
As often you've been told
Well now is the time for action
It's a time for being bold
Time to break with the past
For all that is in yesterday
And today may be your last.

Ron Martin

A Morning Prayer

Dear Lord I thank You
For each day I wake.
Knowing that You care
About me always.
Knowing I shall never be alone
Thank You Lord, for listening
to my innermost thoughts, and
Healing me when I am sick.
For lifting up my spirits
When I am down.
I thank You dear Lord for
Your love and understanding
And the blessings You have given me.
For the joy and peace, the warm
happiness I feel in my heart.
Knowing You are close to me
always.
Protect me each passing day.
Lord I pray
For I need Your love, always.

Doreen Petherick Cox

Lifted

How do you feel when the sun's going down?
Is it a relief that the day's passed around
Or is it a gateway to a new dawn
When you can move forward rather than yawn?

What do you do when the moon passes by?
Sometimes you smile and often you cry
And sometimes you look at your lover and say
Thank you for making a beautiful day.

What do you see in the dark of your room?
No flowers to gaze at, no roses in bloom
But the faint light of stars through the curtains just seem
Like millions of thoughts in many a dream.

So lift up your heart and smile for yourself
The world is so full of a wonderful wealth
Of things that cost nothing to you and to me
Be grateful for fine things, enjoy what you see.

John Cook

1st December

The Cause

Together we can do it.
Together we can fight.
Together we can win.

Alone we can do nothing.
Alone we try in vain.
Alone all will be lost.

Do it together
Or do it alone,
Which is best?

You decide.

Colette McCormick

2nd December

On The Road To Emmaus

(This is a dedication to Br Christian Gisamonyo Fms (my lecturer for Christology))
(Luke 24 v 13:32)

Jerusalem had them disappointed.
The two men had left no time appointed.
They were hurrying home before late
To forget the day and date.
Unknown to the two,
Jesus the Risen joined with them too.
He wanted their version of the narration
Before He added His powerful explanation.
Dusk not asked was end the day
So they asked Jesus if He could stay.
Come the breaking of bread at table
Two men came to recognise Jesus so stable
So was Jesus nowhere to be seen.
The two agreed, 'Returning to Jerusalem is no sin!'
With the gospel they hurried back, armed
To free many in doubts, they were aimed.

Nyasha Musimwa

3rd December

Waking Thoughts

You are my waking thought
Dance into my consciousness
The breaking of the day.

You are my waking breath
Sigh into my flooding mind
The living of the day.

You are my waking smile
Joy into my lightened heart
The hoping of the day.

You are my waking prayer
Speak within my newborn self
Desiring of the day.

John Harding

4th December

Say A Little Prayer

When you're feeling so down and blue
You can't see what you need to do
Say a little prayer
And God will see you through.

When you're feeling so afraid
You don't know how bills will be paid
Say a little prayer
And God will show you a way.

When you're feeling in so much pain
Your daily tasks you can't maintain
Say a little prayer
And God will carry you once again.

His power is mighty and He's aware
Whenever you need someone to care
So offer up a little prayer
And know that God is always there.

Joan Earle Broad

5th December

Precious City

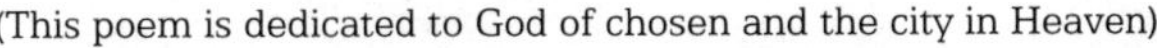

(This poem is dedicated to God of chosen and the city in Heaven)

Exquisite city is lovely in serenity
A city treasure in simplicity
And embellished without complexity
Tranquil and calm in gentility.

Oh! precious city in its picture
Your gentle nature captured in enrapture
Your gem is calm and elegant in pleasure
Splendid in nature and moderate in measure.

A city so unique in its light
Glinting and glittering in the night
The beauty of the city is so bright
Oh! precious city, mighty in its height.

Arharhire Sunday

Dirty Your Knees

Behave like a child,
Live for the present.
Laugh when you're happy,
Shout when you're angry,
Cry when it hurts.

Give voice to your feelings.
Your emotions are valid,
A reflection of truth,
A remembrance of history.

So, dirty your knees,
Tear your clothes,
Mess up your hair,
And behave like a child.

Stephen Hobbs

7th December

Meeting Needs

Lord, when the way seems darkest
And my eyes with tears are dim,
Open my heart to Jesus,
Putting my faith and trust in Him.

Help me to see the goodness, Lord,
In the folks I meet each day,
To overlook any imperfections,
As I greet them along life's way.

Lord, help me to be caring,
So that everything I do,
Meets the needs of someone,
Make me a disciple, good and true.

Malcolm F Andrews

Best Of All

The Saviour called to me
He wanted me to be His own
To live at peace with Him
And never be alone
The Saviour spoke my name
And when I answered to His call
He filled my heart with joy
And loved me best of all.

The Saviour called again,
He wanted me to play my part
And spread His Holy Word
To unbelieving hearts
And if they turn to Him
He will hear them when they call
Then He will take their life
And love them best of all.

The Saviour calls you all
To come and rest beneath His wings
And He will show you all
The wondrous joy His love can bring
So if you walk with Him
He will lead you through the storm
Then He will lift you high
And love you best of all.

Barbara Scriven

9th December

Xanadu Found!

(For the Lockwood Gospel Choir)

Your singing truly lifts my heart, gospel songs from angel's harp,
what a thing of beauty this, sublime words, heavenly bliss,
soul food, I will call it here, talent seen, to me, sincere,
love of love and love of life, banish hurt and painful strife,
awesome gift, so I believe, choral voice, will not deceive,
gives me hope, a fervent wish, sorrow gone with angel's kiss,
doubt me not, none better than, creation of a song that can,
touch the senses, dream I ran, through all women, every man,
if I may, a humble fan, world of ours, a holy plan,
vastest stretch, eternal span, in fervent voice, I sang and sang.

C Thornton

10th December

Fired Up!

('We must assume that there exists a powerful factor outside our globe which governs the development of events in human societies and synchronises them with the sun's activity; the electrical energy of the sun is the superterrestrial factor which influences historical processes' - Chizhevsky 1926 - Russian scientist)

Fired up by cosmic forces and all universal thought,
Am I - a spark that ignites from the source - the one
True flame that burns its glorious way into history. A link
To all that belonged and wishes to become. A life part;
Positive matter that has been charged and found wanting of mind,
Finding its energy, seeking the spirit of place - the destined
Journey where knowing all fires the pulse as one.
My time, my place will be revealed, answered, as questions
Yet untapped, unfold among the ever-increasing expansion
Pushing at the boundaries and borders of the limitless whole.
And I? I shall follow, guided by unseen forces, the influences
And wisdom from others that coexist and who always will.
Guided to reach the illuminated realm of the imagination
Where the flame is fanned to meld with the Creator and to
Create; to exist forever, a vision in the mind's eye. Truly
A vision that encompasses all colours and all hues in obvious
Complementarity. A brilliant rainbow, forged by the conscious
Hand bridging the entire expanse of space/time, knowing
Of every dimension, to last an eternity. Blazing
My trail across the heavens
All can view my soul; then surely all will know:
I exist and am one with the universe -
Fired up by cosmic forces and all universal thought!

Ian Deal

Special Glow

Rising from slumber on this Christmas morn
Sky still and black as could be,
Such brilliant light, pure silver orb
Through my window was beckoning me,

I opened the door, air cold and crisp,
Saw my breath swirl, gazed in awe.
This moon I'd looked at a million times
Never noticed it so bright before.

All was silent, oh sleeping calm,
Felt just like peace on Earth,
'Twas same moon God had created
That shone on His own Son's birth.

In my heart I felt that brighter light
On this Christmas Day's special morn,
Old moon glowed his brilliance
'Tis the day our Saviour was born.

I looked at him, he looked at me
This wondrous circle of light,
He tipped me a wink, it's God's glow I mirror
On this so special day, you're quite right.

Dorothy M Mitchell

12th December

Mother

No more to see your smiling face
Your happy laughing ways
No more to hear your soothing voice
To brighten up our days.
A light went out the day you left
It darkened all our days
But God shows us His reasons in very many ways.
He shows us that the good go first
He needs them most up there
For He has baby angels who need your loving care.
Be happy Mother darling
Your days are now pain free
Give freely of your love and care
The way you did to me.

Jean O'Donoghue

Jesus

I know who holds tomorrow
For I talked to Him today,
I can tell you, His name is Jesus
And He is only a prayer away!

He offers a saving refuge
Shelter from the storm,
He asks no payment for service
Freely grants a sweet reform.

What will you do about Him?
Neutral you cannot be,
Some day your heart will ask you,
'What will He do about me?'

Jesus, the way to salvation
Cast all your care upon Him,
Take His hand, walk with Him daily,
Redeemed, free from all sin!

Pause, here, just for a moment,
Offer the Saviour a prayer,
Reach out your hand to Jesus,
I know, you will find Him there!

Isaac Smith

The Solitary Way

The ways we walked together
Now I walk alone.
No one now to guide me
Through fields and paths unknown.

What joy it was to be with you,
What privilege to share.
But what is it you leave behind?
A broken heart - beyond repair.

What can I do? What is there left
But future's endless days?
Love and joy and hope
Have gone - but sorrow stays.

For you are - where? I am here
And only God can guide.
For man, weak man, can nothing do
To stop the parting tide.

Oh, God Almighty, is it true
And can it really be
That throned in glorious majesty
You care for me?

For if You do, it must be true
My love and I will meet again
With You, in Heaven's home
Where endless love will reign.

Lost soul, take heart and trust in God
For it is He who knows the way.
His hand outstretched, His footstep sure
Follow in faith - and pray.

Jean Bloomer

14th December

Not Alone

Alone in this world,
is that how you are?
Well, if you have Christ
that's better by far.

He'll never leave you,
be close at your side,
there to uphold you,
whatever betide.

In sickness or sorrow,
to Him you can go,
lay hold of His promise,
be sure it is so.

'Lo I am with you,
to end of the age',
His words you will find,
on scriptures' own page.

So walk on with Him,
and seek out His way,
then you'll experience,
His closeness each day.

Coral Raven

Odd Couple?

If I was you and you were me
What an odd couple we would be!

I would be messy, leave my socks on the floor
You'd talk too much and would lay down the law.
I'd play computer games and would always be late
You'd eat salad because you'd be watching your weight.
I'd listen to music and drink cans of beer
You'd watch sad movies, then shed a tear.
I'd give you a hug and squeeze you tight
You'd know that I love you, that we are so right!

If I was you and you were me
What a great couple we would be!

Vanessa Dineen

Seasons

Spring
Early spring sunshine warms the earth
Bulbs reawaken a time of rebirth
Nature's powers flow for all they are worth
What wonders have we yet to behold.

Summer
Warm summer sunshine speeds the growth of the flowers
Brilliant blue skies adorn daylight hours
Nature at the height of her recuperative powers
Engendering colours so bright and so bold.

Autumn
Soft autumn breezes so cool and refreshing
On sun-scorched skin it feels like a blessing
All around the trees are undressing
Leaves turn to red and to gold.

Winter
Cold winter winds and sharp frosty mornings
Dark cloudy skies serve as a warning
High on the hills the snowdrifts are forming
What horrors will nature unfold.

Christine Collins

17th December

On The Way To The Summer Lands

The spirit released from its outer garment,
Rejoices in the freedom of its transient state,
Out through the ether,
To participate in the dance of joy,
Merging with other free spirits,
On a journey of discovery,

Floating randomly and at whim,
Of the conscious mind contained within,
The physical body was but a casket,
Which contained the essence,
A mode of transport for a season,
Cast aside and from which the spirit emerges,

Yet time has no meaning,
When free of earthly restraints,
The spirit,
Moves through many facets of creation itself,
For such are the mysteries that unfold,
In the ever-changing realms of the heavenly abode,

The spirit experiences liberation,
Leaving behind that which restricted its view,
Whilst on earthly pursuits,
Beyond is a place of light and harmony,
Which in its present form, can now be perceived,
Where music transports the soul on its voyage,

Here colours are vibrant and alive,
They stream from the supreme maestro,
Who colours nature in all its glory,
Earth is but a pale reflection in comparison,
The soul returns, to merge with all that is,
On the way to the summer lands.

Ann G Wallace

18th December

Glorious Day!

The sun is up. Another glorious day begins.
Time to step out and cast away old sins,
To climb a mountain, walk along a beach,
Strive to achieve things far beyond my reach.

To love all men, of every race and creed,
And cleanse myself of selfishness and greed.
From this day on to make each moment real,
And every task, pursue with honest zeal.

To reach these goals, I can no more delay,
No dwelling on mistakes of yesterday;
But strive each day to love my fellow man,
And share with all the Lord's eternal plan.

On that day when *my own* sun does not rise,
I pray my friends, you'll see it through my eyes,
And think of me as one who strove to fully live,
Each glorious day the good Lord had to give.

Brian Croft

Season

Spring, summer, autumn, winter,
Beloved of painter, poet and printer,
Nature's faithful first quartet
The great Creator did beget;
Colour-changer, harvest-grower,
For the reaper and the sower
Gathering all our needs for living,
For which all should express thanksgiving
And rest assured as ages come,
Each spring will bring continuum.

Yet wait! There's more than this to scan
With stress, much less u-top-ian,
In season's varied repertoire,
That lives and land alike doth mar:
Heatwaves, freeze-ups, floods and droughts,
Disasters, famines, fears and doubts
That such excess could stem from Heaven,
Unless of course 'twere Karma-driven,
Explaining why Earth's climate sequel,
Appears to be dispersed unequal.

So! do we here delight or drag
Through some anomalous lucky bag?
Are climate's favoured scenes pre-set,
For those who own the means? And yet
Dilemmas come not, without horns,
Nor grows a rose without its thorns,
Accept then! nature's changing climate,
Great metamorphosis in-fi-nite,
Defying time and rhyme and reason,
And yet we simply call it *season.*

Alexander Jamieson

The Folk Of Yesteryear

As the lights go on this Christmas,
Bringing happiness and cheer,
My memory drifts to days gone by,
And the folk of yesteryear.

When a party was a party,
What joyful times we had,
We would raise a toast in happy song,
And get the feeling that life's not bad.

It was a time I took for granted,
Because it happened every year,
But now I long to turn back time,
To the folk of yesteryear.

Perhaps my comfort comes from knowing,
That we can never be apart,
For when a soul has touched your spirit,
Their love lives on within your heart.

Wendy A Lyon

20th December

A Step In The Dark

I had travelled this road many times before,
But as I made my way today,
A thick swirling fog made travelling a chore,
It felt like the world had gone away.

Nothing familiar, no landmarks I find,
In all directions I see only grey.
With nothing to see I feel I am blind,
I worry, has the world gone away?

I have an important decision to make,
Should I go or should I stay?
I know that there is a lot at stake,
What if the world has gone away?

With courage I take that first step in the dark,
But first I kneel to pray.
Now I need to look beyond the mark,
Believing the world has not gone away.

Marjorie Brown

The Shortest Day

From my kitchen window I can see
A lone pheasant wandering quietly
Nasturtium blooms in this December hour
My beloved fuchsias still flower

On this the shortest day, antirrhinums
Compete with lovely red chrysanthemums
From the hedge a small pink rose nods to me
While the mallows are blooming profusely

The weatherman promised a cold snap soon
Then we shall face a dose of winter's gloom
But it won't be long before I can say,
'I saw the first snowdrop in bloom today.'

Valerie Ovais

Winter

The landscape transformed
To a wonderland of white
The earth covered in snow
Is an incredible sight.

The countryside has changed
And is seen in a new way
Winter beauty surrounds
Things I pass every day.

Stark skeletal branches have
Been clothed without sound
This magical world reveals
Animal tracks on the ground.

An impression of my footprint
Makes me feel as though
I am first to walk this
Path in the virgin snow.

This white protected covering
Shows a vulnerability, I find
As the world has been transformed
So has my troubled mind.

A chance to start again
In a world so clean and bright
Like having a blank canvas
This time to get it right.

Moon Stone

Sound Of Safety

Listen to the sound of safety,
This will be your skill,
The silent splash of raindrops,
Falls to your window sill.

My little drop of genius,
A reminder of myself,
A photographic future,
Sits smiling on my shelf.

The glass within my window,
Rebellious in its panes,
Transparent in its nature,
They want to walk again.

And I will wish to follow,
The freedom in their minds,
I cannot find their pathway,
To them my sight is blind.

But sunlight hits my face,
It is gleaming down my cheeks,
The voice is smooth and calming,
And within the rain it speaks.

Listen to the sound of safety,
This will be your skill,
The silent splash of raindrops,
Falls to you window sill.

Gabrielle Conway

22nd December

Peace Of Mind

Peace is a sense of deep contentment we rarely know,
More easily captured by a round of wordy prose.
We all seek this state during our spell on Earth
'Til the time we leave from the day of our birth.

Though not our prime aim in early years,
It soon assumes importance in life's vale of tears.
We may attain this calm in different ways
As we learn to survive the rapids of testing days.

Some may never know this blissful state,
As time after time some crisis is their fate.
Yet such is the strength of Man's enduring hope,
He strains everlastingly in his efforts to cope.

Let us all enjoy peace!

A Jessop

Home

When you leave your place of work, your school or field of play,
A familiar phrase may pass your lips, 'Goodbye, I'm on my way',
Wherever your departure's from, at the end of each day's roam,
When you say, 'I'm on my way', you're mostly going to your home.

We often take for granted, that home is always there,
And standing by the fireside, will be your comfy chair,
There for you to take your ease, and rest your weary head,
And enjoy some quiet moments, until it's time for bed.

How often have you heard it said, it's nice to be at home,
Whether with a family, or sometimes just alone,
You can do the things you want, in your own kind of way,
Or just enjoy the memories of what occurred that day.

People go on holiday, seeking sun and golden sands,
Or enjoying scenes of beauty, in far-off pleasant lands,
They may tell of the stories, from wherever they did roam,
Then you often hear them say, 'It's nice again to be back home'.

Home is said to be your castle, be it large or small,
And you can be a king or queen, when behind your castle wall,
Of all the many things in life, and the pleasures Man has known,
Can you find one to compete, with the place that is your home?

Donald Futer

The Miracle Of Christmas

A brilliant star lights up the sky
People travel from far and wide,
To be by a special baby's side.
Away from Herod they hide,
Heeding a heavenly guide.

Mary and Joseph gaze upon their child,
With pride in each other's eyes.
Listening to His soprano cries,
Knowing He will grow into a king of the wise.
This Saviour, will win humans' kindness first prize,
And rid the world of sin when He dies.

He fulfilled His destiny
Now the world is a better place.
Thanks to Him,
Evil will eventually cease
And the good will be on the increase.

This is the meaning of Christmas,
It's because of Jesus!
And arrives in our winter's season,
For a very holy reason.

Ali Sebastian

The Way It Is

There is no end
There's no beginning
Who we are
We'll always be
The only thing that ever changes
Is how we see the way it is

See the world through
Different eyes
There's part of you
That never dies
Don't ever be afraid to die
That's not the way it is

The way it is, is hard to see
But seeing it, will set you free
The way you are, will always be
That's the way it is

And in the end
You're just beginning
Who you are
You'll always be
All that ever really changes
Is how you see the way it is

The way it is, is hard to find
But finding it will free your mind
Love is here for those who see
That's just the way it is.

Allie Roberts

Newborn

At midnight
I will lift
The baby Jesus,
Give him a kiss
And place Him in the crib.
Once more I will welcome Him,
Tiny babe,
With deep thankfulness and joy
To my home, to my life, to my heart.
His radiance
Fills the dark places,
Gives cause for hope,
And when all else fails,
Transforms my world.

Anne P Munday

24th December

Needing God's Herald Angels Again

O Father, we pray You to wing Your angels' flight
To all areas of this globe's hurt, hate and wrong priority
That stand to stifle the course of Man's future pathway
May they stop us in our tracks to seek fulfilment of Your glory
Bringing us to the life of Heaven to show the ways to change
Yielding with tears of repentance and compassionately outstretched arms
        In Your love - above all
Draw closer to us Father, through their Holy presence
That we shall cease forever, losing our way so sadly
Motivating us to live creatively, as You designed so purposely
Let us feel Your guidance, healing, grace and mercy
Inspiring all men to treat each other in value and respect
Determined to make their future one of blessings and real progress
        In Your love - above all
How we need You now, Father, as never before in history
Calling out for Your angels of light and joy to Earth again
Swift in their earnest flight of special urgency and purpose
That Your planet's people's commitments together shall be refreshed
That nations shall willingly share in the best of common aims
To become the caring family You so wanted us all to be
        In Your love - above all
        And forever - blessed.

Don Harris

25th December

The Reason For The Season

It's not the baubles on the fir trees,
That are making children smile,
Nor the glitter on the cards, or the cold freeze
That shows it's all worthwhile.

It is not the stockings loosely hung
On the edge of bed posts,
Or gaily coloured presents for old and young,
Which people buy at any cost.

Neither the kissing under the mistletoe,
Can be the reason for gaiety and joy,
And children playing in cold, wet snow,
Could account for this 'feeling' they all employ.

It's not the raging music that makes you want to dance,
Or the fashion-crazy people who stay up late at night.
Though the wine is wholesome, and the women take a chance,
To find the ideal partner before the year has flown full flight!

The reason for the season
That brings out all this 'love',
Is that *Jesus*, our Saviour, was born,
Sent by God from Heaven above.

Jesus wants us to celebrate,
His birth, His life, each Christmastide,
No need to have to wait,
Jesus is the reason for the season, in Him we shall abide.

Hilarie Grinnell

Christmas

The bells are ringing out their message,
Telling us all it's Christmas morn.
We fill the church to offer our thanks
For that far off day when Christ was born.

Carols, curling up the columns,
Blend with the organ in their flight,
Filling the high, echoing spaces,
Descending on coloured shafts of light.

Our children gather around the stable,
Built in the corner with loving care.
None noticing the fallen flower,
Blood-red, forgotten - lying there.

Gwen Hoskins

The Gift Of Life

Precious! Wholesome! Right from the start.
Gracious! Spectacular! Oh magnificent art!
You were made with such motivational chamber,
In you I see the world's greatest treasure.

Oh gift! Oh life! Such awesome formation.
So colourful! Diverse! Earth's vibrant companion.
With hands and feet you take great steps,
Like heads and shoulders you interconnect.

'Who could have designed this magnificent art?'
In whose splendour and beauty we cannot depart.
Oh what a gift that the giver should give;
For with this gift we were made to live.

This gift is given for all to use;
The young, the old, it's for you to choose.
Cherish it, mould it, let it work for you,
Live it, love it, it's the best thing to do.

Julliet Miller

26th December

Awesome Silence

An awesome silence covers lately fallen snow.
Midnight now, the day that Christ was born so lowly,
For us the stillness blanketed with orange glow,
Two thousand years reflected down have gone so slowly.
Dense and murky fog does mark this birthday holy.
Black blood hangs down on pointed holly,
Marking years of human folly.

So still the night; this holy night.
A snow-topped lawn that bears no breath of sound,
Nor slightest movement from the icy ground.
The snow has lightly traced each twig of lace;
Gives frozen burden to each arching conifer within
This silent enclosed garden, that recedes to fog's obscurity.
The past unrecognised. An unknown future with no face.

Standing here on solid step,
Nothing, absolutely nothing, sways this night-time peace.
A moment for reflection. Gaze upon the world we've made.
If every spot on Earth were coated in preserving icy fog,
Perhaps we could begin again and set another course.
Take up a new philosophy, where violence and anger
Have no part. Give place to help and generosity,
With love to all humanity.

My feet upon this earth grow cold,
Now midnight's passed, I feel a trembling quiver,
And through my bones there spreads a premonition's shiver.
This man-made world has surely had its day.
What must it take to wash it all away?
A new belief to banish old,
Where help for suffering neighbour is the need.
Mankind at last can prove his singularity of breed.

David Light

Jesus 'Is' ...

Injured I lay on my lonely road,
Hoping someone would heed my cry.
Had thought my friends would see me soon,
They did - then passed me by.
What did they think as there I lay?
Couldn't they see my deep despair?
They made assumptions then walked away,
Not one turned back to care.
I'd seen their priestly garments,
Felt hopeful as they drew near.
But they didn't want to see me,
Nor did they wish to hear.
Someone despised and rejected
Came close by me to kneel.
To take my hand and love me,
Someone my heart could heal.
He drew me close and closer,
In His heart I found my rest.
In Him is all I've sighed for,
My friend and He's my best.
        Jesus 'is' ...

Rosie Hues

27th December

Advent Candle

Watching and meditating
as the candle burns.
How your flame at times grows tall
pushing upward, struggling
as we sometimes struggle
on our journey through life,
to reach further and give more light.
A light in our darkness
soothing our fears,
bringing us nearer to God,
calming our souls.
Watching as each number
disappears in melted wax,
soon all will be gone.
Let God's love be constant.
As this year draws to a close
and a new one begins,
let there always be a light in our lives,
reaching up like the flame,
showing us the way ahead,
to be sure and firmly set on our journey.

Sheila Park

The Christ Child Is Waiting For You

The wise men have gone back to the east
Savouring sweet memories of perfect peace
Yet war and famine forever remain
The world needs to find that star again
Whose ray points every year anew
To the One who was born to die for you
Come to the cradle, come if you are able
The Christ Child is waiting for you

The shepherds have gone home to the hill
Their joy complete, their hearts are still
Yet death and darkness forever remain
In a world so tired of sin and pain
God lights the pathway out of danger
Through the star which guides you to the manger
So come to Him now and humbly bow
The Christ Child is waiting for you

W Campbell

A Passing Thought

A passing thought - it's been a while
A present bought - a nice warm smile
A distant choir - a winter's night
Logs on the fire that's burning bright
A lovely sight - a cosy glow
The ground is white outside with snow
A nice warm room with songs of praise
They went so soon these good old days
A nice hot drink - a home-made roast
A friendly wink - the smell of toast
We made the most of what we'd got
As I would boast - 'I've got the lot!'
A treasured gift to remember
As hearts would lift each December
Our friends ran round to have a look
At new toys found - and each new book
A festive cheer - a Christmas wish
As it draws near I reminisce
The taste of mints - a sip of port
And nice hot drinks - a *passing thought*
There's candlelight - as logs burn bright
One lovely sight - a winter's night
In Granny's home there was such bliss
The years have flown - I reminisce
Frothy Horlicks - custard biscuits
Pick 'n' mix - then Weetabix
Then we would go and rest our heads
On our pillow in cosy beds
Nights of pleasure those winters bought
Nights I'll treasure - a passing thought ...

Paul McIntyre

29th December

Confusion

Does the road through life seem like a maze
Lots of paths and different ways?
Do we often in confusion travel
With tangled thoughts to unravel?

Like a tide with ebb and flow
Torments of tomorrow come and go.
Trust in the Lord, there is a way
Amid confusion, calm of day.

Margaret Godsman

30th December

Golden Times

Golden times are gone so soon,
Radiant in their dawning's moon,
Shining with their twinkling rays,
Brightening life's fleeing days.

Golden times are over quick,
Only memories can stick,
Whilst the days, like hurricanes,
Go whirling on through joys and pains.

Golden times bring tears of joy
To glad hearts that they employ,
And over then, they fly away,
But they return another day.

Golden times can know no end,
All through your life they are a friend,
New year bells peal out their joy,
Ringing in for girl and boy.

Golden times, though gone so soon,
Are radiant in their dawning's moon,
Shining with their twinkling rays,
Brightening life's fleeing days.

Alison Lingwood

Altercation

Some people live day to day
Without a care in the world.

But what about our world?
Have you ever looked outside
And seen the death all around us?

Did you ever stop to think about
What was going on outside your door?

But you just don't seem to care
As others help save our planet
From the destruction caused from war.

How can you sit there and say you don't see it
When it's there outside your door?
Don't you even care?

Those who care about making a difference
Care enough about living
Help make the difference.

There are people dying
Even in our own land
So how can you sit there denying
When our children are out there dying?

Help save the world we live in
Heal it from our ignorance
Make it better for all who live in it
Save it for our children.

We'll make a difference
Somehow we will find a way
As long as people care
There is no wrong way
To help make a difference.

Andrew Ball

31st December

New Beginnings

Another year gone by
A new page is turned
Mistakes were made
And many lessons were learned

We can't turn back that page
But move forward we must
Set foot upon the right path
In our instincts, we should trust

We, ourselves, know what we need
Deep down, within our hearts
But getting to the finish line
We're bound to find false starts

Take each day and set your goal
Then try hard to achieve
But don't feel down, if all is lost
In you, you must believe

Anne Elibol

Tomorrow

Clouds fill the sky;
Your life darkens and the world disappears;
Everything becomes totally meaningless.
- But, as with time, the clouds will pass and
  reveal the sun which was there all the time.

As you look into the sunlight, your face
  shines again whilst your shadow appears behind you.
The future beckons as you hold out a
  nervous and shaking hand.
One step at a time
  - one day at a time
Slowly but surely your strength will grow
  and slowly but surely life will grow.

There was a time when every day seemed like yesterday
But there will come a time when today greets tomorrow;
When your mirror becomes a window;
It is then that you will see your future
  and not reflect on the past.

Have faith, have courage and have hope
  for you *will* survive.

Derek Dobson

Daily Reflections 2006

A to Z of Authors

A to Z of Authors

A Boddison 353
A Cooper 185
A J Brooking 76
A Jessop 502
A Teesdale 205
A Yap-Morris 186
Adeola Oluwadamilola Adekoya 334
ADMT 280
Alan Bruce Thompson 464
Alan Millard 454
Alan Pow 15
Albert Watson 361
Alexander Jamieson 496
Ali Sebastian 504
Alison Adams 394
Alison J Mannion 139
Alison Lingwood 517
Alison Mitchell 389
Alison Shields 201
Allie Roberts 505
Alvin Creighton 348
Amelia Petherick 453
Andrew Ball 518
Angela Cutrale Matheson 192
Angela R Davies 103
Anjum Wasim Dar 306
Ann G Wallace 494
Ann May Wallace 202
Anna Bacon 373
Anna Powell 466
Anne Elibol 519
Anne Gray 258
Anne Hadley 450
Anne Marie Latham 446
Anne P Munday 506
Anne Sackey 309
Anne Veronica Tisley 249
Anne-Marie Ryan-Tucker 124
Annie Frame 134
Annie R Harcus 17
Annoha Kyeremeh 346
Anonymous 404
Anthay 57
Anthony J Brady 278
Anthony J Gibson 379
Arharhire Sunday 481
Ashley O'Keefe 159
Avis Nixon 193
Azariah Ephratah 292
B G Clarke 31
B W Ballard 223
Bakewell Burt 222
Barbara Finch 283
Barbara Holme 298
Barbara Jean Whelan 363
Barbara Rumsey 22
Barbara Scriven 484
Benjamin Takavarasha 110
Bernard Brady 166
Bernard Brown 271
Beryl Elizabeth Moore 30
Beth Izatt Anderson 308
Betty Mason 119
Betty Mealand 87
Bill Hayles 398
Bill Newham 323
Bob Lowe 68
Bob Tose 93
Brenda Artingstall 207
Brenda Maple 426
Brenda W Hughes 467
Brian Croft 495
Brian Frost 267
Brian Strand 281
Brigid Smith 98
Bryn Phillips 176
C M Armstrong 329
C R Slater 356
C Thornton 485
Carla Iacovetti 217
Carol Ann Darling 111
Carol Bosisto 88
Carole Herron 254
Carole Morris 105
Caroline Baker 256
Caroline Pybus 24
Caron P Simpson 100
Cath Powell 71
Cathy L Kaiser 53
Cathy Mearman 288
Catriona Toland 200
Charlie Kwame Maguire (14) 369
Chiang Yee 405
Chris Whooley 203
Christina Earl 417
Christina Miller 300
Christine Blackburn 240
Christine Collins 493
Christine Hardemon 400
Christine Naylor 46
Christine Potts 196
Christine Renee Parker 25
Clare Price 175
Clive Cornwall 338
Colette Horsburgh 37
Colette McCormick 477
Colin Wallace 318
Coral Raven 491
Craig Brown 72
D Huff 171
D W Hill 247
D Wakefield 424
Dan McPheat 458
Daphne Cornell 54
David Cameron 469
David Charles 44
David Gasking 277
David Light 511
David M Walford 330
David Radford 322
Davide Trame 268
Davis Akkara 408
Debbie Evans 409
Debbie Nobbs 137
Deborah Gail Pearson 406
Deborah Hall 420
Dee Gordon 145

A to Z of Authors

Deirdre Wise	266	Emma Bacon	211	Hilarie Grinnell	508
Denise Watson	121	Emma Jane Glenning	419	Hilary Ayling	97
Derek Dobson	520	Emmanuel Petrakis	174	Hugh J Lynch	152
Derek Norris	286	Enid Gill	140	I Millington	70
Derek Sones	55	Enid Hewitt	234	Iaian W Wade	294
Des Beirne	173	Enid Rathbone	472	Ian Bosker	165
Di Bagshawe	29	Eric McCrossan	429	Ian Deal	486
Diana Daley	418	Erica Morley	385	Ian Russell	163
Diana Morcom	206	Estelle James	257	Idris Woodfield	386
Diana Mudd	382	Eugene Dunkley	237	Ilan Micah Block	172
Diana Price	188	Eve Kimber	388	Imogene Lindo	357
Divyamaan Srivastava	221	Finnan Boyle	104	Irene Corbett	253
Don Harris	507	Fiona Geelan	251	Isaac Smith	489
Donald Futer	503	Fiona Jo Clark	305	J Brohee	230
Donna Hardie	412	Firecloud	170	J F Grainger	313
Doreen Petherick Cox	475	Frances Walker	102	J Flanagan	214
Doreen Ranson	182	Françoise de Pierpont	191	J Johnson	208
Doris E Pullen	395	Frank Howarth-Hynes	296	J P Henderson-Long	158
Doris Hoole	189	Fred Brown	232	J W Whiteacre	151
Dorothy Ledger	314	Gabrielle Conway	501	Jac Simmons	157
Dorothy M Kemp	99	Garry Bedford	73	Jacqueline Taylor	423
Dorothy M Mitchell	487	Gary Stephenson	226	James McConalogue	36
Doug Cairns	471	Geoff Lowe	231	James Michael Thomas	282
Duchess Newman	457	George Carrick	183	James R Lucas	26
Duncan Robson	61	George Terry	49	James Stephen Thompson	381
E B Wreede	51	Gertrude Schöen	335	James Walsh	133
E L Hannam	78	Gillian Humphries	229	Jamie Caddick	460
E M Gough	291	Gladys Bruno	413	Jan Bevan	213
E Osmond	85	Glenda Stryker	445	Janan Robin Zaitoun	149
Edward Brookes	444	Glenys Harris	28	Janet L Stephenson	343
Eileen M Lodge	187	Gordon Harper	21	Janet Rocher	177
Eileen Martin	138	Grace Divine	228	Janice Ginever	96
Elaine Day	295	Graham Watkins	264	Janice Melmoth	74
Elaine Donaldson	255	Grant Kinnaird	118	Jasmina Trifunovic	43
Elaine Phillips	80	Greeny	414	Jay Berkowitz	75
Eleanor Anderson	435	Greta Robinson	42	Jean Bailey	344
Elizabeth Bruce	181	Gwen Hoskins	509	Jean Bloomer	490
Elizabeth Hiddleston	411	H W Gosling	275	Jean Caldwell	198
Ella Mae Agnew	95	Hannah Yates	194	Jean Jackson	345
Ellen M Lock	197	Hayes Turner	470	Jean Martin-Doyle	65
Elma Heath	242	Hazel Sheppard	160	Jean McPherson	244
Elsie G B Horrocks	362	Heather Ferrier	316	Jean O'Donoghue	488
Emily Thommes	269	Helen M Clarke	367	Jean P McGovern	312

A to Z of Authors

Jean Wood 407
Jeanette Gaffney 462
Jennifer Davey 35
Jennifer René Daniel 368
Jessica E Stapleton 162
Joan Brooks 18
Joan Constantine 310
Joan Earle Broad 480
Joan Green 199
Joan Heybourn 190
Joan May Wills 336
Joan Prentice 34
Joan Winwood 320
JoAnn P Kelly 47
Joanne Hale 455
John A Mills 270
John Clarke 461
John Cook 476
John Davies 63
John Gowans 354
John Harding 479
John Harrison 260
John Neal 79
John Pegg 155
John Robinson 425
John Warren 66
John White 380
Jolanta Gradowicz 50
Jonathan Covington 342
Josephine Foreman 236
Josh Brittain 195
Joy Saunders 219
Joyce Beard 33
Joyce Hockley 289
Julia Eva Yeardye 112
Julia Pegg 263
Julliet Miller 510
June Davies 238
K E Harrod 350
K Windsor 204
Karen Eberhardt-Shelton 89
Karen Lewis 56
Kath Gay 141
Kathleen Scatchard 328
Keith L Powell 109
Keith Wright 415
Kenneth Mood 60
Kevin Baskin 449
Kevin McNulty 377
Kevin Welch 227
Kim Mehaffy 126
Kimberley Otter 311
Kirk Antony Watson 358
L E Growney 38
L Goldsmith 123
Leanne Mizen 122
Lee Mak 48
Leigh Crighton 101
Liam Bagnall 349
Lilian Pickford-Miller 58
Linda Barnard 287
Linda Knight 265
Lindy Roberts 67
Lisa Wolfe 210
Lorna Lea 125
Lorna Tippett 106
Lorna Troop 384
Louise Pamela Webster 82
Louise Wheeler 130
Lydia Barnett 39
Lyn Sandford 243
Lynda Arnold 452
M Butcher 225
M Courtney Soper 224
M Cubis 169
M Dawson 430
M Osmond 456
M Ross 468
M Spence 359
Maggie Cartridge 465
Maggie Dennis 64
Malcolm F Andrews 483
Malcolm Williams 156
Margaret Ann Wheatley 153
Margaret Anne Hedley 117
Margaret Findlay 274
Margaret Godsman 516
Margaret McGinty 147
Margaret Parnell 387
Margaret Ward 233
Marian Bythell 216
Mariana Zavati Gardner 52
Marie Butler 438
Marion Schoeberlein 325
Marjorie Brown 498
Marjorie Busby 45
Marjorie Leyshon 20
Marjory Price 365
Mark Murphy 383
Marlene Parmenter 285
Mary Guckian 331
Mary Hudson 447
Mary Hughes 164
Mary May Robertson 473
Mary Rafferty 167
Mary Thompson 378
Mary Tickle 340
Mary V Ciarella Murray 451
Maureen Boyd Joines Anderson 403
Maureen Powell 437
Maureen Quirey 319
Mavis Johnson 180
Melissa Halidy 372
Michael Boase 259
Michael Denholme Hortus Stalker 107
Michael Rowson 120
Michele Amos 154
Michelle Harvey 69
Mick Nash 332
Mike Green 421
Mollie D Earl 391
Molly Ann Kean 62
Moon Stone 500
Muriel I Tate 209
N Ferguson 293
Nadine Mackie 366
Nancy Reeves 392

A to Z of Authors

Nava Semel 442
Neil C Roper 396
Nicola Barnes 341
Norma Griffiths 463
Norma Jean Johnson 272
Norman Bissett 290
Norman Dickson 439
Nyasha Musimwa 478
Octavia Hornby 303
Oritsegbemi Emmanuel Jakpa 416
P Ellis 273
P M Peet 375
P P Christodoulides 128
P T Barron 374
Pamela Carder 422
Pamela Constantine 142
Pat Geeson 321
Pat Heppel 443
Patricia B Spear 144
Patricia M Farbrother 459
Patricia Patterson 148
Patricia Raisôn 337
Patricia Rose Thompson 301
Patricia Turpin 347
Paul Kelly 339
Paul McIntyre 515
Pauline E Reynolds 83
Pauline Pickin 246
Peggy Courteen 241
Penny Kirby 113
Penny Miller 261
Pete Robins 448
Peter Buss 402
Peter Davies 297
Peter G H Payne 146
Philip Worth 179
Phyllis Bowen 235
Phyllis Wright 302
R Bateman 390
R S Wayne Hughes 116
Rachel E Joyce 431
Rachel Hall-Smith 434
Rachel Leivers 108
Ray Smart 427
Richard Gould 161
Richard Hain 41
Rita Scott 129
Robert S Dell 114
Robert Waggitt 352
Robin Morgan 178
Roger N Taber 212
Roland Seager 184
Roma Davies 441
Ron Beaumont 304
Ron Martin 474
Rosemary E Pearson 150
Rose-Mary Gower 92
Rosie Heartland 250
Rosie Hues 512
Rowland Patrick Scannell 370
Ruth Blaug 410
Ruth Clarke 440
Ruth Daviat 279
Ruth M Ellett 433
Ruth Toy 32
S Beverly Ruff 239
S M Thompson 436
S Mullinger 284
Sam Kelly 16
Sara Crump 360
Sarah Stephenson (16) 245
Sean I Riley 324
Sean Kinsella 327
Sharon Townsend 262
Sheila Macdonald 276
Sheila Park 513
Shirley Ballantine 428
Shirley Gwynne 252
Shirley Ludlow 127
Shirley Perkins 81
Sigurd Ramans-Harborough 307
Simon Peterson 218
Stein Dunne 59
Stephen Hobbs 482
Steve Matthews 248
Steve Prout 131
Steven Pearson 317
Sue Cann 23
Susan Geldard 333
Susan Latimer 401
Sylvia Scoville 315
T D Green 220
T G Bloodworth 143
Teresa Garfield 86
Teressa Rhoden 376
Terry Godwin 326
Terry J Powell 19
Tessa Jane Lee 77
Tina Sanderson 135
TJR 136
Tom Fox 115
Tom Ritchie 94
Tony Bush 371
Tracey Lynn Birchall 27
Tracie Rhodes 299
Trevor Reynolds 399
Trudie Sullivan 355
V E Godfrey 84
Valerie Hall 132
Valerie Ovais 499
Vanessa Dineen 492
Vaughan Stone 90
Vera Collins 91
Victoria Morley 215
Vineta Svelch 40
Vivek P Sarma 397
Vivien Steels 393
W Campbell 514
Wendy A Lyon 497
Wendy Dedicott 364
Will A Tilyard 168
Wilma G Paton 432
Winifred Curran 351

Triumph House

We hope you have enjoyed reading this book - and that you will continue to enjoy it in the coming years.
If you like reading and writing poetry drop us a line, or give us a call, and we'll send you a free information pack.

Write to:
Triumph House Information
Remus House
Woodston
Peterborough
PE2 9JX
Tel: 01733 898102
Email: info@forwardpress.co.uk